WHAT'S IN A NAME?

The origins of station names on the London Underground

by Cyril M. Harris

Published in co-operation with
London Transport by
Midas Books Limited

CONTENTS

	Page
Acknowledgements	2
Introduction	3
Map of the London Underground	4
What's in a Name?	5-93
Names of Underground Stations now closed	94
Bibliography	94-96

ACKNOWLEDGEMENTS

The author would like to thank: The publicity staff of London Transport for their help. The County Archivist Essex County Council, Miss Diana Daniels of Mill Hill for her expert typing, London's many librarians for their assistance, Charles E. Lee for checking the numerous transport dates; my mother, Mrs. Hilda Harris, for her many hours of reading and checking proofs. And, finally, a number of unknown London citizens for their help and assistance.

First published in Great Britain by Midas Books in association with London Transport in 1977.

Text in 9/10pt Times
© Midas Books/London Transport
Text Cyril M. Harris 1977 and 1979
Second (revised) edition 1979
ISBN 0 85936 185 3

Printed by McCorquodale (Newton) Limited
Newton-le-Willows, Merseyside

INTRODUCTION

Like many Londoners I sit (or stand) most days on one of the London Underground trains and besides reading my newspaper, look at the boards displaying the routes of the different lines and wonder how the stations obtained their names. Why is Leicester Square so named when it is so far from Leicester? Why is Tottenham Court Road many miles away from Tottenham? Is there any connection (besides the one by train) between Canons Park and Cannon Street?

Many spellings and pronunciations of the words relating to place names change in the course of history and some have different meanings and interpretations in different areas. Bearing this in mind, I have endeavoured to use the names that are generally accepted for each entry in this book.

Opening dates of stations shown at the end of each entry record the introduction of passenger services by London Transport or its predecessors.

What's in a Name? gives the name origins and the history of all the stations on the Underground and I hope you, like I, will wonder no more how these names originated.

C.M.H. London 1976

Every effort is made to ensure that the information given on station opening and closing dates are correct, but the opinions expressed and the explanations are those of the author, not of London Transport or Midas Books.

MAP OF THE LONDON UNDERGROUND

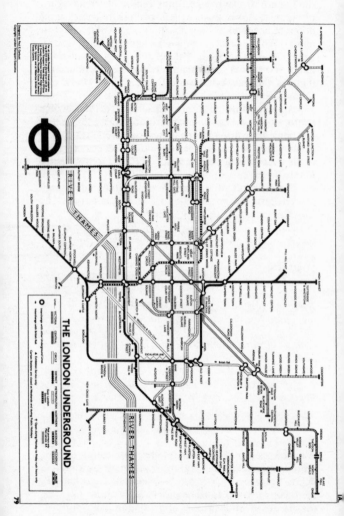

THE LONDON UNDERGROUND

4

Acton Town was recorded as *Acton(e)* in 1181 and the name is derived from the Old English *ac*, 'oak' and *tun*, 'a farm'—meaning 'the farm by the oak tree'. There was a busy little village in this area from the 16th century onwards developing into the *town* of *Acton*. It has been known as Church Acton to distinguish it from East Acton, formerly a separate hamlet.

The station was built as Mill Hill Park and opened on 1 July 1879; rebuilt and opened still as Mill Hill Park on 20 February 1910; but renamed Acton Town on 1 March 1910.

Aldgate is named after the gate which once spanned the road between Dukes Place and Jewry Street. The original gate was built by the Saxons and the name is derived from *Aelgate*—meaning 'open to all' a free gate. It has also been interpreted as the *old-gate* but this is probably incorrect. *Aldgate* was one of the original four gates in the City Wall, was rebuilt in 1609 but was finally demolished in 1761.

The station was opened on 18 November 1876; reconstructed and opened on 10 June 1926.

Aldgate East—see Aldgate.
The original station was opened on 6 October 1884. It was resited farther east and the new station was opened on 31 October 1938.

Aldwych. It is said that the Saxon King Alfred the Great (reigned 871-899) when he finally occupied London allotted territory to the Danes, whom he had just conquered, as a settlement here. The name is derived from the Old English, *eald*, 'old' and *wic*, 'a village'—means 'the old village' and it seems that a dairy farm was established here by the Danes. The area was recorded as *Aldewich* in 1211 and was known to

the beginning of the 17th century as *Via de Aldewyche*
now represented by Drury Lane. *Aldwych Lane*
survived as Wych Street until 1903 when the then
London County Council renamed it *Aldwych,* the
present street passing near the site of the old lane.

The station was opened as Strand on 30 November
1907 and renamed Aldwych on 9 May 1915.

Alperton originally *Ealhberhington,* was recorded as
Alprinton in the 12th century and the name is derived
from the personal name of the Saxon *Ealhbeart* and
Old English *tun,* 'a farm'—means 'the farm of
Ealhbearht' and his family who once lived on a site
here. It is sometimes recorded that Alperton is derived
from 'apple farm', but this can be discounted. The
name changed to *Alperton* in the course of time.

The station was opened as Perivale-Alperton on 28
June 1903 and renamed Alperton on 7 October
1910.

Amersham was recorded as *Agmondesham* in 1066
and the name is derived from the original wording
Ealgmundsham being the personal name of the Saxon
Ealgmund, and Old English *ham,* 'a
homestead'—means 'the home of Ealgmund' and his
family who once lived on a site here. Changed to
Amersham *c.* 1675.

The station was opened on 1 September 1892.

Angel. This district and road junction at the end of City
Road takes its name from a once famous coaching inn
that dates from at least 1638.

The *Angel* was one of the commonest mediæval inn-
signs for in the mid-18th century there were 23 Angel
Alleys and 30 Angel Courts in London. The building
now stands empty and little noticed on the corner of
Pentonville Road and Islington High Street. The only
indication of its past history is *Angel Mews,* that runs
behind the building.

The station was opened on 17 November 1901.

Archway. In 1813 the Archway Road was constructed to avoid the slope up to Highgate Hill. The viaduct was designed by Sir Alexander Binnie and built in 1897 over the road in place of the former *Highgate Archway*. The district is, therefore, known as *Archway*. Railings, seven feet high, were erected on the viaduct to discourage the many suicides that took place here, but the view is still spectacular.

The station was opened as Highgate on 22 June 1907 and renamed Archway (Highgate) on 11 June 1939, Highgate (Archway) on 19 January 1941, and Archway in December 1947.

Arnos Grove was recorded as *Arnold(e)s Grove* in 1551 and it seems that the name should be associated with the 14th-century family of Margery *Arnold* who once lived in this area and, therefore, this district of North London is so named. The *Grove* itself runs to the north of the nearby Arnos Park.

The station was opened on 19 September 1932.

Arsenal takes its name from the famous *Arsenal Football Club* which moved here in 1913 from Woolwich where it had been founded at the Royal Arsenal Factory in 1884—hence the nickname for the team: The Gunners.

The station was opened as Gillespie Road on 15 December 1906 and renamed Arsenal on 31 October 1932 at a pre-war height of the Club's fame.

Royal Exchange (Bank)

B

Baker Street was completed in 1799 and was named after (1) Sir Edward *Baker* of Ranston in Dorset who was the owner of an estate in the area, or (2) possibly Sir Robert *Baker* the Bow Street Chief Magistrate who helped quell the riots at Queen Caroline's funeral in 1821. The street is, of course, associated with the famous fictional detective Sherlock Holmes 'who had rooms at 221b Baker Street'.

The Metropolitan Line station was opened on 10 January 1863, the 'extension' line Station on 13 April, 1868, and the Bakerloo Line station on 10 March 1906.

Balham was known as *Baelenham* in 957 and later as *Bealganhamm* being derived from the personal name of the Saxon *Bealga,* and Old English *ham,* 'a homestead'—means 'the home of Bealga' and his family who once lived on a site here. It was recorded as *Balgaham* in *c.* 1115.

The station was opened on 6 December 1926.

Tate Gallery (Pimlico)

Bank takes its name from the *Bank of England* which was established in 1694 based on the proposals of William Paterson, a Scotsman. From 1694–1724 the business of the Bank was carried on at Mercers' Hall, and then at Grocers' Hall. In 1724 a site in Threadneedle Street was purchased; the building was erected in 1732–4 and rebuilt in 1940. 'The Bank' has the nickname *'The Old Lady of Threadneedle Street'*; this has been attributed to Sheridan or William Cobbett.

Threadneedle Street was recorded in 1598 as *Three needle Street*; this probably refers to (1) a tailor's sign, for this area was once an enclave of tailors and drapers, or (2) a children's game *'threadneedle'*, first noticed in 1751 but may be two centuries older. There is no evidence that the street was ever the centre for the Needlemakers' Company.

The Waterloo & City Railway was opened by the Duke of Cambridge on 11 July 1898 which was the 50th anniversary of the opening of the original Waterloo Station.

The City Station was called City, although sometimes referred to as Mansion House. It was not renamed *Bank* until 28 October 1940.

The Northern Line station was opened on 25 February 1900, and the Central Line station on 30 July 1900. The reconstructed station was opened on 5 May 1925. The Bank–Monument subway was opened on 18 September 1933.

Barbican was called *barbicana* when a Roman Tower once stood just north of the street that now bears this name. *Barbicana* is Latin in origin and, in its turn, is probably from the Persian wording meaning 'upper chamber'. The Saxons named the tower *burgh kennin*—meaning 'town watchtower', on which for many centuries fires were lit to guide travellers to their destinations across London. It seems the tower was pulled down in 1267 on the orders of Henry III but it was then rebuilt in 1336 on the orders of Edward III.

The date when the tower was finally demolished is
uncertain but it is known there was a house on the site
in 1720. The area has been extensively redeveloped
since the second World War as the *Barbican Project.*

The station was opened as Aldersgate Street on 23
December 1865; renamed Aldersgate & Barbican
1923, and Barbican on 1 December 1968.

Barking was recorded as *Berecingum* in 735 and is
named (1) from the Saxon people the *Bercia* and the
Old English place name word ending *ing,* literally 'the
people who lived at'—Barking, we can deduce,
means—'the home of the Bercias'. The area was
divided into various manors during the Middle Ages,
one being *Berengers* a variation on the original name.
(2) It is also possible that the name can be interpreted
as 'the dwellers among the birch trees' and, maybe,
this referred to the Bercias.

The station was opened by the London, Tilbury &
Southend Railway on 13 April 1854 and first used by
Underground trains on 2 June 1902.

Barkingside was so named in 1538 being on the
extreme edge of the old parish of Barking. The word
side is associated with a slope or hill especially one
extending for a considerable distance, which was no
doubt the case during the 16th century.

The station was opened by the Great Eastern
Railway on 1 May 1903 and first used by Underground
trains on 31 May 1948.

Barons Court. Unlike Earl's Court this name has no
connection with the law, or the nobility, but was so
named after an estate that extends from the District
Line to Perham Road to the south. The estate was
planned by Sir William Palliser and built at the end of
the 19th century. The name was fabricated—perhaps
in allusion to the title of *Court Baron* then held by the
Lord of the Manor or because Earl's Court was the
name of a nearby district.

The station was opened on 9 October 1905.

Bayswater was recorded as *Bayard's Watering* in 1380 and has had many variant spellings before being named as *Bay(e)swater* by 1659. The original *Bayard's Watering* was the place where the Westbourne Stream crossed the Oxford Road (now Bayswater Road) and is possibly derived from the *Bayard* family who once lived in this area.

The station was opened as *Bayswater* on 1 October 1868. Later known as Bayswater (Queen's Road) and then Queen's Road, Bayswater. Renamed Bayswater (Queen's Road) & Westbourne Grove on 20 July 1922. Reverted to Bayswater in 1933.

Becontree as the name suggests takes its name from a local natural feature although associated with the Saxon people the *Beohha* who had an encampment by a distinctive tree, which was probably a boundary mark, recorded as *Beuentreu* in Domesday Book. It is possible, however, that the name is from Old English, *beacen-treo(w)*, 'beacon tree' being an old meeting place.

The station was opened as Gale Street by the L.M.S. railway on 28 June 1926; renamed Becontree 18 July 1932. Used by Underground trains from 12 September 1932.

Belsize Park was recorded as *Balassis* in 1317 from the Old French wording *bel asis*—means 'beautifully situated' and was no doubt aptly named from the manor house and park which were once on the present site of Belsize Square. No fewer than ten streets, in this part of north west London, include *Belsize* in their name.

The station was opened on 22 June 1907.

Bethnal Green. *Blithehale* was the recorded name for this district during the 13th century. The second element *hale* means—'an angle or corner of land'.

Maybe *Blithe* is (1) a corruption of the personal name *Bathon* (or *Blia*), a family who resided here in the reign of Edward I (1272–1307) or (2) perhaps refers to an ancient stream of this area called *Bythe*. The 'village green at Bathon's river meadow' could be the complete meaning of the name. Has had many changes of spelling until recorded as *Bethnal Greene* in 1657. On what remains of the *Green* now stand St. John's Church (built in 1825–8), the Bethnal Green Museum and the local public gardens.

The station was opened on 4 December 1946.

Blackfriars. This area takes its name from the colour of the habits worn by the friars of a Dominican monastery who were known as the *Black Friars*. The monastery was established during the 13th century by the Earl of Kent, but was closed on the orders of Henry VIII in 1538. Part of the building later became the *Blackfriars Theatre* which was eventually pulled down in 1665.

The station is built on the site of Chatham Place which was named in honour of William Pitt, 1st Earl of Chatham, and was opened on 30 May 1870.

Blackhorse Road was recorded as *Black House Lane* in 1848 which is the correct spelling, for the road takes its name from an old *Black House*, being on the site of an old Clock House. Changed to *Blackhorse Lane* (then road) at a later date, this change has some connection with the Cockney dialect.

The station was opened on 1 September 1968.

Blake Hall in the parish of Bobbingworth takes its name from the early 18th-century house, which has been since 1789 the home of the Capel-Cure family. The building has twice been extended, in 1822 and during the 1840s. The Library was used as an R.A.F. 'Operations Room' during 1940–8; from the nearby airfield flew planes fighting the Battle of Britain.

The station was opened by the Great Eastern Railway on 24 April 1865 and first used by Underground trains on 18 November 1957.

Bond Street was laid out in 1686 to designs by Sir Thomas *Bond,* Comptroller of the Household of Queen Henrietta Maria (The Queen Mother), and is named after him, although he died in 1685. The street is now renowned for its fashionable shops and picture-dealers' galleries. The south portion of the street is known as *Old Bond Street,* being renamed in 1734, while the north portion running to Oxford Street is known as *New Bond Street,* named in 1732.

The station was opened on 24 September 1900.

Borough. This district is part of ancient London, for here the Romans founded a settlement and built a 'high street' as an approach road to London Bridge. The *Borough* is a small part of Southwark and although the word borough means 'a fortified place' (Old English *burh*) the word now has another definition. It also refers to a town with its own local government, for in the late Middle Ages this was the only London Borough outside the City Wall and sending its own Member to Parliament, and has kept its name ever since.

The station was opened on 18 December 1890.

Boston Manor. This *Boston* has no connection with its more famous namesakes in Lincolnshire or the U.S.A. Known during the 14th century as *Bordeston* from *Bords* (a personal name) and Old English *tun,* 'a farm'—means 'Bords farm', which in its turn has been corrupted to *Burston,* then *Boston* during the 16th century. The *Manor* originally belonged to the convent of St. Helen's Bishopsgate and its ownership has changed hands many times during the course of history. *Boston Manor* is noted for its Tudor and Jacobean Mansion—'Boston House'.

The station was opened on 1 May 1883 as Boston Road, renamed Boston Manor on 11 December 1911, and the rebuilt station was completed 25 March 1934.

Bounds Green is a district of North London whose name is derived from its association with the families of John le *Bonde* in 1294 and Walter le *Bounde* during the 13th century and being recorded as *le Boundes* in 1365. *Bounds Green* is the modern version of the name. Nothing is left of the *Green*, the area now occupied by the Bounds Green Road.

The station was opened on 19 September 1932.

Bow Road. This main road is so called from (1) an arched ('bow') bridge built over the River Lea in the 12th century; or (2) from the *bow* (or bend) in the road to the east of the station, which can still be seen just before one arrives at the modern fly-over.

The station was opened on 11 June 1902.

Brent Cross takes its name from the nearby river that joins the Thames at Brentford and was recorded as *Braegente* in 959. In its turn the river-name is derived from the hypothetical Old English *Brigantica*, probably meaning the holy or high river and as the river flows mostly through low country the former is most likely. The name became *Brent(e)* by the 13th century.

The station was opened as Brent on 19 November 1923 and renamed Brent Cross on 20 July 1976.

Brixton is recorded as *brixges stane* in 1062, as *Brixistan* in Domesday Book and the name is derived from the personal name of the Saxon *Beorhtric* and the Old English *tun*, 'a farm'—means 'the farm of Beorhtric' and his family that once lived on a site here. The name changed to Brixton in the course of time.

The station was opened on 23 July 1971.

Bromley-By-Bow was recorded as *Braembelege* in 1000, *Brambeley* in 1128 and is derived from the Old English *broom* (tree(s)) and *leah,* 'a forest'—means (1) 'the forest where the broom trees grew' or can be interpreted as (2) 'the clearing among the brambles'. The second part of the name is self explanatory—see Bow Road for origin.

The station was opened by the London, Tilbury & Southend Railway on 31 March 1858 as Bromley. It was first used by Underground trains on 2 June 1902 and was renamed Bromley-By-Bow on 5 May, 1968.

Buckhurst Hill, as the name suggests, takes its name from a local natural feature, recorded as *(1a) Bocherst(e)* in 1135 from the Old English *beech* (tree) and *hyrst,* 'a copse' or 'wood'—means 'the wood of beech tree(s)', later to be called *Buckhurst.* The area has also been called *Goldhurst,* the 'gold' referring no doubt to the colour of the trees in the wood. The *Hill* refers to another nearby feature.

The station was opened by the Eastern Counties Railway on 22 August 1856 and first used by Underground trains on 21 November 1948.

Burnt Oak. Tradition has it that the Romans had a site near here which they used as a boundary mark where fires were lit as a guide—so a *burnt oak.*

The station was opened on 27 October 1924.

Bushey & Oxhey. Both these names are derived from local natural features. *Bushey* was recorded as *Bissei* in Domesday Book and with variant spellings in the course of time. It has two derivations both having the same basic meaning (1) *'Bissei'* from the Old French *boisseie*—means 'a place covered with wood' and (2) from the Old English *byse,* 'bush, thicket', and *haeg* 'enclosure'—means 'an enclosure protected by thicket'. Nearby *Oxhey's* name origin is very similar, recorded as *Oxangehaege* in 1007—means 'enclosure for oxen', changed to *Oxhey* by the 17th century.

The station was opened as Bushey by the London & Birmingham Railway in May 1844, but was first served by Bakerloo Line trains on 16 April 1917. The station was renamed Bushey & Oxhey in December 1912, then renamed Bushey in May 1975.

Caledonian Road was constructed *c.* 1826 and is named from the *Caledonian Asylum* for Scottish children established on a site nearby in 1815. The road was referred to as the 'New Road from Battle Bridge to Holloway' in 1841.

The station was opened on 15 December 1906.

Camden Town. This area of north west London was built *c.* 1791, and was once a manor belonging to St. Paul's Cathedral. The manor was obtained, by marriage, in 1795 by Charles Pratt, Earl of *Camden*, of Camden Place in Kent, and is so named. The Earl allowed his land to be leased for building houses, so in the course of time *Camden Town* came into use.

The station was opened on 22 June 1907.

Cannon Street has no connection with guns or even billiards as the name might suggest, for the candle-makers and wick-chandlers who made their wares for the Church, lived here in the late Middle Ages. First mentioned in the records of *c.* 1180 as *Candelwrichstrete* (from *Candle* and Old English *wic*, 'a dwelling') which is self explanatory. Through a series of name-shortenings and the Cockney dialect the name was contracted to *Cannon Street* by the mid-17th century and this modern form was noted by Pepys in his famous diary in 1667. On the site of the present main-line station was once the Steelyard, a store to which members of the German Hanseatic League once brought their goods for sale.

This station was opened on 1 September 1866. The Circle Line station was opened on 6 October 1884.

Canons Park. Six acres of this area were granted to the Prior of the St. Augustinian canons of St. Bartholomew's, Smithfield, in 1331 and were recorded as *Canons* during the 16th century. *Canons Park* later became the property of the Duke of Chandos and on the estate was built the Duke's magnificent mansion also named 'Canons' which was demolished after its sale by the Duke's heir in 1747, being broken up and sold by lots at auction. Today part of the site is occupied by the 'North London Collegiate' school for girls.

The station was opened on 10 December 1932.

Carpenders Park is part of this residential area north of London. It takes its name from the 14th-century family of Simon le *Carpenter* and was recorded as *Carpenters Hill* in 1556.

The station was opened by the London & North Western Railway on 1 April 1914. Closed from 1 January 1917. It was reopened for Underground trains on 5 May 1919, but not used again by the L.N.W.R. until 10 July 1922. The station was resited on 17 November 1952.

Chalfont & Latimer. Two origins of the name *Chalfont* have been recorded but both are of a similar nature. Noted as *Ceadeles funta* in 949 from (1) the personal name of a Saxon, *Ceadel* and Old Welsh *funta*, 'a spring or stream'—means 'Ceadel's home near a spring', or (2) more simply from Old English *char*, 'rock stone' and (again) *funta*—means 'the stony stream' from a once nearby natural location. *Latimer* is also derived from a personal name, recorded as *Isenhampstede Latyer* in 1389, which takes its name from William *Latymer*, who obtained the manor on this site in 1330; the name was finally shortened to *Latimer*.

The station was opened as Chalfont Road on 8 July 1889 and renamed Chalfont & Latimer in November 1915.

Chalk Farm. It has been suggested this is a corruption of the wording *Chalcot Farm* but there is no evidence that a farm ever existed in this area. Recorded as *Chaldecot(e)* in 1253, which was an old village. It is stated that this name is derived from *cold cottages* referring to the slopes of nearby Haverstock Hill which were bleak and exposed in the early days of settlement in this area. It seems that there was also a place of shelter here for travellers to London.

The station was opened on 22 June 1907.

Chancery Lane was constructed by the Knights Templars *c.* 1160 and has a long history with many changes of name. It was recorded as Newstrate (New Street) in the early part of the 13th century. During the reign of Henry III (1216–72) a house was erected on the eastern side of the lane for the conversion of Jews to the Christian faith. The house became famous and Newstrate became *Convers Lane.* Towards the end of the 13th century, Edward I banished the Jews from the country and the house was used by 'the Keeper of the Rolls', where the official records of the Inns of Chancery were kept and once again the name of the street was changed to *Chancellor's Lane* and was recorded as this in 1320. Eventually this name was superseded (once again) by *Chancery Lane, c.* 1454 and it seems to imply that the Chancellor (of the Rolls) had a personal office or residence in the Lane.

The station was opened on 30 July 1900. After extensive reconstruction, a new station was opened on 25 June 1934.

Charing Cross Embankment. By tradition, it is said that Edward I in 1291 set up a stone cross near what is now the courtyard of the main-line station to mark the last resting place of the funeral cortege of his Queen Eleanor as it passed from Harby to Westminster— hence the *Cross* part of the name which was recorded as the *stone cross* of *Cherryngge* during the 14th century. There was a little village here named

Cyrringe c. 1000 and the name is derived from the Old English *cierring,* 'turning' or 'to turn', probably referring to the bend in the river Thames nearby. *Charing Cross Road* was built in the 1880s. The Embankment, is the roadway by the River Thames. In 1863 an Act of Parliament was passed for the building of the embankments and work stated immediately on the new *Victoria Embankment* between Westminster and the Temple. It was completed and opend to the public in 1870.

The District Line station was opened as Charing Cross on 30 May 1870. The Bakerloo Line station, opened on 10 March 1906, was first named Embankment; renamed Charing Cross (Embankment) on 6 April 1914, when the Northern Line platforms were opened. The combined stations were named Charing Cross on 9 May 1915. It was renamed Charing Cross Embankment on 4 August 1974, and further renamed as Embankment on 12 September 1976. A new Charing Cross station will be opened on the site of Trafalgar Square Station and the former Strand Station.

Tudor Buildings (Chancery Lane)

Chesham had an early association with the Old English word *ceaster*—signifying 'a Roman town and fortification'. Recorded during the 10th century as *Caesteshamm* from the Old English *ceastel*, literally 'a heap of stones', and *hamm*, 'a water meadow'—meaning 'a boundary mark by a spring'. In the course of time the name has changed to *Chesham*, and nearby is the river Chess.

The station was opened on 8 July 1889.

Chigwell was recorded as *Cingheuuella* in Domesday Book and maybe is associated with a Saxon named *Cicea*. But the name is probably derived from (1) Old English *ceaege*, 'gorse' and *weg*, 'well' or (2) the very similar—*chingle*, 'shingle', and (again) *weg*—means very simply 'the well within the shingle', which has changed in the course of time to *Chigwell*.

The station was opened by the Great Eastern Railway on 1 May 1903 and first used by Underground trains on 21 November 1948.

Chiswick Park. Recorded as *Ceswican c.* 1000, *Chiswick* has various spellings throughout time, is derived from the Old English *cese*, 'cheese' and *wic*, 'dairy farm'—means 'a cheese and dairy farm' from a once nearby location. Changed to *Chiswick* in the course of time.

The station was opened as Acton Green on 1 July 1879; renamed Chiswick Park & Acton Green in March 1887; and Chiswick Park on 1 March 1910.

Chorleywood. The Old English word for a free peasant lower than the rank of nobleman was *ceorl* and these people once had an encampment on a site near here. Recorded as *Charlewoode* in 1524 although the name is of an earlier origin and is derived from the Old English *ceorl* (the group name of the people) and *leah*, 'a wood'—means 'the wood or clearing of the free peasants' and known as *Chorley Wood* by 1730.

The station opened as Chorley Wood on 8 July 1889,

and the recognized modern spelling of Chorleywood
is used on Underground maps. It was renamed Chorley
Wood & Chenies in November 1915.

Clapham Common. There was an ancient village on the
site of the present *Clapham,* recorded as *Clopeham* in
Domesday Book. The name is derived from the Old
English *clap,* 'a hill' and *ham,* 'home'—this wording for
hill usually refers to one on stubby ground—means,
simply, 'the home(s) on the hill'. The *Common* was
called *Clapham Common* in 1718 and the meaning of
the word is—a track of open land used in *common* by
the inhabitants of the town.
   The station was opened on 3 June 1900.

Clapham North—see Clapham Common.
The station was opened as *Clapham Road* on 3 June
1900 and renamed *Clapham North* 13 September
1926.

Clapham South—see Clapham Common.
The station was opened on 13 September 1926.

Cockfosters. This district of north London was
recorded as *Cockfosters* in 1524 and although the
origin of the name is uncertain, it is possible that it is
derived from either of the following: that *Cockfoster*
was in fact the personal name of a family that once lived
here, or there was in fact a house on the edge of Enfield
Chase in 1613 called *Cockfosters* and it is suggested
that this was the residence of the chief *forester* (or *cock
forester*), hence this rather unusual name.
   The station was opened on 31 July 1933.

Colindale was recorded as *Collyndene* in 1550, *Collins
Deepe* in 1710 and probably should be associated with
the family of a John *Collin* who once lived here. The
'Deep' must refer to the valley of the nearby Silk
Stream (later changed to *Dale,* from the Old English
dael, 'a valley'). *Colindale,* therefore, means 'the

home of the Collins Family in the valley'.

The station was opened on 18 August 1924.

Collier's Wood. Very little can be said about this name that is taken from the *Colliers* or 'charcoal burners' who worked in this area during the 16th century. The *Wood* was once a nearby natural location.

The station was opened on 13 September 1926.

Covent Garden was originally the walled enclosure and garden belonging to the monks of Westminster Abbey, recorded in 1491 as *Convent Garden* (from Old French *couvent*), which stretched from Long Acre to the Strand. After the dissolution of the monasteries the site was claimed by the Crown, sold to the 1st Earl of Bedford in 1552 who had a house built here, while the 4th Earl had the area laid out as a residential quarter. *Covent Garden* was famous for its fruit market established in 1661, now moved to a site at Vauxhall in south London, and for its Royal Opera House, the third one on this site which was built in 1858.

The station was opened on 11 April 1907.

Croxley. The name is derived from the Old English *crocs,* 'a clearing' and *leah,* 'a forest'—means 'the clearing in the forest'. It was recorded as *Crokesleya* in 1166 with variant spellings until 1750 when it was known as *Crosley (Green).*

The station was opened as Croxley Green on 2 November 1925 and renamed Croxley, 23 May 1949.

D

Dagenham East. The name *Dagenham* was originally recorded as *Daccanhamm* in 692 and is derived from the personal name of the Saxon *Daecca* and the Old English *ham,* 'a homestead' and means 'the home of Decca' and his family, that once lived on a site here. It was recorded as *Dakenham* in 1254.

The station was opened as Dagenham by the London, Tilbury & Southend Railway on 1 May 1885, and was first used by Underground trains on 2 June 1902. It was renamed Dagenham East, 1 May 1949.

Dagenham Heathway—see Dagenham East.
The *Heathway* as the name suggests takes its name from the road that runs to the north, through Dagenham to Becontree Heath.

The station was opened as Heathway on 12 September 1932 and renamed Dagenham Heathway in May 1949.

Debden takes its name from a natural location of the area and is recorded as *Deppendana* in the Domesday Book. It is derived from the Old English *deb,* 'deep' and *den,* 'valley'—which means simply 'the deep valley'. It was recorded as *Depeden* in 1227.

The station was opened by the Great Eastern Railway as Chigwell Road on 24 April 1865, and renamed Chigwell Lane on 1 December 1865. It was again renamed as Debden on 25 September 1949, when it was first used by Underground trains.

Dollis Hill was recorded as *Daleson Hill* in 1593 but the name origin is unknown; possibly it is taken from a nearby manor that was once here and some suggest that the family came from *Dawley*. *Dollis Hill* Lane, the main road, climbs the *Hill* at this point.

The station was opened on 1 October 1909.

E

Ealing Broadway. *Gillingas* was recorded for this area *c.* 698 and is derived from the Saxon people the *Gilla* and the Old English place name word ending, *ing,* literally, 'the people who lived at'—means 'the home of the Gillas'. Has had many changes of spelling—*Ilingis c.* 1127, then *Yealing* to *Ealing* in 1622. The *Broadway* is the main road beside the station.

The District Line station was opened on 1 July 1879.

Ealing Common—see Ealing Broadway.
The *Common* lies to the south of the station—see under Clapham Common for meaning of 'common'.

The station was opened on 1 July 1879 as Ealing Common; renamed Ealing Common & West Acton in 1886; and reverted to Ealing Common on 1 March 1910.

Earl's Court. After the Conquest the De Vere family were granted the Manor of Kensington which at one time had a *court* house. Later the head of the family was created Earl of Oxford, hence the name the *Earl's Court.* The old Court stood beside a little lane which is still called Old Manor Yard, but the court building was demolished in 1886. Now on the site are Barkston and Bramham Gardens.

The station was opened on 31 October 1871, burnt down 30 December 1875 and repaired temporarily; new station further west opened 1 February 1878.

East Acton—see Acton Town for meaning of name.
East Acton was formerly a separate hamlet from Acton and was recorded as *Estacton* in 1294.

The station was opened on 3 August 1920.

Eastcote was known as *Estcotte* during the 13th century and the name is only slightly changed in the course of time. The name is derived from the Old English *cote*, 'cottage' or 'shelter'—means 'the cottage(s) to the east', literally the hamlet to the east of Ruislip, for there was once a Westcott during the 18th century.

The station was opened on 26 May 1906.

East Finchley—see Finchley Central.
The station was first used by Underground trains on 14 April 1940.

East Ham was recorded as *Hamme* in 958 which signifies that this and West Ham was then one single geographical location and not until 1206 was the name *Eastham* recorded. The name is derived from the Old English *hamm*, 'a water meadow'—referring to the low-lying riverside meadow near the bend of the Thames.
(see also **West Ham.**)

The station was opened by the London, Tilbury & Southend Railway on 31 March 1858; first used by Underground trains on 2 June 1902.

East Putney—see Putney Bridge.
The station was opened on 3 June 1889.

Edgware was recorded *AEgces Wer* in 972–8 and *Eggeswera* later and is derived from the personal name of a Saxon *Ecgis* and *weir*—means very simply, 'Ecgis', fishing pool from a local stretch of water. From an early set of boundaries the precise position of the fishing pool can be ascertained; it is where Watling Street (now Edgware Road) crosses the Edgware Brook. It appears as *Edgware c.* 1495.

The station was opened on 18 August 1924.

Edgware Road was once part of the Roman road called *Watling Street* that ran from Dover through London to St. Albans. During the 18th century the road became

Edgware Road, being the direct route from Marble Arch to Edgware, which lies to the north west.

The Metropolitan Line station was opened on 10 January 1863; the Bakerloo Line station on 15 June 1907.

Elephant & Castle is named after an old tavern which was originally on the site of a 16th-century playhouse, the 'Newington Theatre', which staged many of Shakespeare's plays. Later converted into a tavern and, during the 18th century, to a posting house and inn, being rebuilt in 1816 and again in 1898. The tavern had a gilt model of an *elephant and castle* on its frontage, which was preserved when the building was demolished in 1959, and is now displayed in the nearby shopping centre. The sign originated from the badge of the Cutler's Company who adopted the elephant as its device in 1445 when at the marriage of Henry VI to Queen Margaret the members of the Company wore elephants as decorations upon their coats or shields; this may have represented the ivory used by cutlers for their craft. The theory that the name is a corruption of *The Infanta of Castile* has no historical foundation. The present day 'pub' stands a short distance from the old site and belongs very much to the 1970s.

The Northern Line station was opened on 18 December 1890; The Bakerloo Line station on 5 August 1906.

Elm Park, as the name suggests, takes its name from natural local woodland and was perhaps a meeting place of the local inhabitants long ago.

The station was opened on 13 May 1935.

Embankment—see Charing Cross Embankment.

Epping was recorded as *Eppinges* in the Domesday Book from the people known as the *Yippinga*, derived from the Old English *yppe*, 'a raised place' and the *ing* word ending (literally 'the people who lived here') and means 'The people who live on the uplands', referring also to a look-out post they had here. It was recorded as *Upping* in 1227, then *Epping*.

The station was opened by the Great Eastern Railway on 24 April 1865 and first used by Underground trains on 25 September 1949.

Euston takes its name from the main-line station, opened on 20 July 1837, which was adjacent to Euston Grove and Euston Square on the estate held by the Duke of Grafton, whose seat was at *Euston Hall,* Suffolk.

The station was opened on 12 May 1907, and completely rebuilt between 1961 and 1968.

Old Curiosity Shop (Holborn)

Euston Square was laid out in 1805 and, like *Euston,* takes its name from the seat of the Duke of Grafton. The station, which was on the site of a farm which existed as late as 1830, was opened as Gower Street on 10 January 1863 and renamed *Euston Square* on 1 November 1909.

F

Fairlop. A legend surrounds the name of Fairlop. In the early part of the 19th century there was a fine oak tree here, which sheltered a long-established fair founded by a certain Daniel Day. When Day died in 1767 his friends, after much consideration, decided to make his coffin from the tree and as the tree continued to flourish, they agreed that they had made a *fair lop*. A little fanciful perhaps, but the name is derived from *fair* and the Modern English *lop* 'a small branch or twig'—and means 'the beautiful trees with their leafy branches' which stood nearby.

The station was opened by the Great Eastern Railway on 1 May 1903 and first used by Underground trains on 31 May 1948.

Farringdon. This part of central London takes its name from *Farringdon Street*. In 1279 the City merchant William *Farendon* of the Goldsmiths' Company purchased the 'ward' of this area and became an Alderman of it two years later; the street was named in his honour. The street was built in 1738 upon arches, above the old River Fleet which is now a sewer.

The station was opened on 10 January 1863 as Farringdon Street; renamed Farringdon & High Holborn 26 January 1922; became Farringdon on 21 April 1936.

Finchley Central was recorded as *Finchelee-leya* c. 1208 and it is possible that the name is derived from (1) what can be interpreted as a *finch clearing* (meaning the bird) and the Old English *leah*, 'a forest'—means 'the clearing in the forest with the finches'. (2) More likely the wording is from a personal name, *Finc*—meaning 'Finc's Forest'. The name has many spellings and was recorded as *Fyncheley* in 1547.

The station was opened by the Great Northern Railway as Finchley & Hendon on 22 August 1867; it became Finchley (Church End) on 1 February 1894, and Finchley Central on 1 April 1940; it was first used by Underground trains on 14 April 1940.

Finchley Road. In 1827 an Act of Parliament was passed to build a new road out of London to Barnet, to avoid the hills of Hampstead and Highgate. This road was planned by way of *Finchley*—hence the name, although the site of the station is some miles to the south of Finchley itself.

The station was opened on 30 June 1879.

Finsbury Park is on the site of the earlier *Hornsey Wood*. The Park, opened in 1869, was so called because the inhabitants within the old Parliamentary borough of Finsbury initiated a movement for its acquisition, which all seems very curious since it is far from Finsbury, which is near central London. *Finsbury* itself was recorded as *Vinisbir* in 1231 and this is most likely to have been derived from an Anglo-Scandinavian name *Fin*, and the Old English *burgh*, 'manor'—and thus means 'Fin's Manor'. It was recorded as *Fenysbury* in 1535.

The station was opened on 14 February 1904.

Fulham Broadway. The manor of *Fulanham* is recorded as early as 691. There has been much speculation about the origin of the name, two explanations being—(1) *foul-town* on account of its muddy ways near the river or (2) *fowl-ham*—being the haunt of wild-fowl. Both of these explanations can now be discounted. It is more likely that *Fulham* is derived from the personal name *Fulla* and the Old English *hamm,* 'a water meadow', being descriptive of the low-lying bend in the River Thames at this point—means 'The Meadow where Fulla lives', referring to an early Saxon and his family. Has had many changes in spelling and recorded as *Fullam* in

1533. The *Broadway* is the main street beside the station.

The station was opened as Walham Green 1 March 1880; renamed Fulham Broadway 2 March 1952.

Westminster

Gants Hill recorded as *Gantesgave* in 1291 and the name may well be associated with the family of Richard le *Gant.*

The station was opened on 14 December 1947.

Gloucester Road was known as 'Hog moore lane' as late as 1858 and at this time was probably descriptive of a muddy tract. Was renamed in the early 19th century after Maria, Duchess of *Gloucester,* who lived in the road at the turn of the century.

The station was opened as Brompton (Gloucester Road) on 1 October 1868; renamed Gloucester Road 1907.

Golders Green was recorded in 1612 and *Golder* seems clearly to refer to a personal name although no such recorded name has been noted in the early history of the parish. It seems that the name should be associated with John le *Godere* in 1321 and John *Godyer* of Hendon in 1371 and it may well be that *Golders* is a corruption of the later name. It is also suggested that *Godyer* was an obscure farmer who in fact sold his property and left the district. The *Green* was once part of the fields of Middlesex, which remained rural until the arrival of the railway.

The station was opened on 22 June 1907.

Goldhawk Road was *Gould Hawk* Lane in 1813 and maybe the road should be associated with a family named *Goldhawk(e)* of the 15th century, for the name is frequently mentioned in 'Court Rolls' of this time. There was also a *Goldhauek* living in nearby Chiswick as early as 1222.

The station was opened on 1 April 1914.

Goodge Street was once called 'Crab tree field', being a
meadow belonging to a widow named Mrs. Beresford
who married a Marylebone carpenter, John *Goodge*
c. 1718. When the street was built *c.* 1770 the name
was taken from William and Francis *Goodge* who then
owned the site.

The station was opened as Tottenham Court Road
on 22 June 1907; renamed Goodge Street 9 March
1908.

Grange Hill. *The Grange* was one of the manors
originally belonging to Tilty Priory. After the dissolution of the monasteries it was granted in 1537 to
Thomas Adlington; it changed hands many times until
the manor was given as an endowment to Brentwood
Grammar School in 1558. The School retained the
property until the late 19th century when the land was
sold and the building demolished. The *Hill* is the road
at the front of the station.

The station was opened by the Great Eastern
Railway on 1 May 1903 and was first used by
Underground trains on 21 November 1948.

Great Portland Street. In 1710 the manor of
Marylebone was bought by the Duke of Newcastle, but
by 1734 it passed to the Second Duke of *Portland.*
When the street was built in the late 18th century it was
so named in honour of the Duke, the northern part
being known as *Portland Road,* which was recorded in
1793. The prefix *Great* does not indicate the impor-
tance of the street itself but that there are smaller
streets of the same name in the neighbourhood.

The station was opened as Portland Road on 10
January 1863 and renamed Great Portland Street
1 March 1917.

Greenford was recorded as *grenan forda* in 845 and as
Greneford in the Domesday Book. As the name
suggests, it refers to a *ford,* which was a crossing place
over the River Brent which led to a *green.*

The station was opened by the Great Western

Railway on 1 October 1904. A new station for Underground trains was opened on 30 June 1947. The G.W.R. station was closed on 17 June 1963.

Green Park was created in 1668 and extends north to Piccadilly; it is 53 acres in size and triangular in shape. Originally added to the Royal Parks by Charles II, it replaced St. James's Park as the fashionable resort of society. Reduced in size by George III in 1767 to enlarge the gardens of Buckingham Palace, it was then known occasionally as Upper St. James's Park. The name seems to have been derived from the *green* grass that 'grew all around'.

The station was opened as Dover Street on 15 December 1906 and renamed Green Park 18 September 1933.

Gunnersbury. Tradition has it that on a site near here stood the dwelling of *Gunhilda* (or *Gunyld*) the niece of the Danish King Canute (reigned 1016–1035) but this seems to rest on unsupported evidence. Recorded as *Gounyldebury* in 1334 its name seems to be derived, nevertheless, from a female name of Scandinavian origin—*Gunnhild's* (or variations) and the Old English *burh,* 'a manor'. It was recorded as Gunsbury in *c.* 1651.

The station was opened by the London & South Western Railway as Brentford Road on 1 January 1869 and renamed Gunnersbury on 1 November 1871. First used by Underground trains on 1 June 1877.

Hainault is not of French origin as it may seem, but is a corruption of the earlier name *Hyneholt*. In its turn this is derived from the Old English *hiwan,* 'a household' and *holt,* 'a wood' (or *hale,* 'a nook of land')—means 'the household on the land with a wood'. The household no doubt refers to a local religious community. The modern spelling seems to arise from a fictitious connection with a Philippa of *Hainault*.

The station was opened by the Great Eastern Railway on 1 May 1903. First used by Underground trains (after reconstruction) on 31 May 1948.

Hammersmith was recorded as *Hammersmyth* in 1294 and was a hamlet within Fulham until 1834. The origin of the name is in doubt. Some suggest that it is derived from (1) Old English *ham,* 'a home' or 'town' and *hythe* 'a port'—means 'the home by the port', referring to its location on the Thames, or (2) more likely from (again Old English) *hamor,* 'hammer' and *smydde* 'a smithy'—referring to a local blacksmith who once lived here. It was recorded as *Hammersmith* in 1675.

The Hammersmith & City Line station was opened on 13 June 1864, and resited farther south on 1 December 1868. The District Line station was opened on 9 September 1874; burnt down 20 January 1882; rebuilding completed 23 August 1882.

Hampstead is a name of simple meaning being derived from Old English *ham,* 'a home' and *stede* 'a site'—meaning, literally 'the home-site', and probably refers to a farm-site. Recorded as *Hemstede* in the 10th century and *Hamstede* in the Domesday Book. The spelling has hardly changed throughout the centuries.

The station was opened on 22 June 1907.

Hanger Lane was named *Hanger Hill* in 1710 and marks the site of a wood recorded as *le Hangrewode* in 1393 and is derived from the Old English *hangra* 'a wooded hill' with clinging steep slopes, later changed to *Lane.*

The station was opened on 30 June 1947.

Harlesden was recorded as *Herulvestune* in Domesday Book and comes from the personal name of the Saxon *Heoruwulf* (or *Herewulf*) and Old English *tun*, 'a farm'—means 'Heoruwulf's farm', being on a site where he and his family once lived. It was recorded as *Herlesdon* in 1291.

The station was opened by the London & North Western Railway on 15 June 1912 and first used by Underground trains on 16 April 1917.

Harrow & Wealdstone—for *Harrow see* Harrow-on-the-Hill. *Wealdstone* was *Weald Stone* in 1754 and the name may have derived from (1) John atte *Stone* (13th century) or John Stute de *Stone* (16th century) who lived in this area or (2) more probably from the Old English *weald*, 'a forest', indicating that the land here was once covered by the heavy Middlesex woodlands, and a 'boundary stone'. A 'stone', three feet tall, still stands outside the 'Red Lion Hotel' but it is doubtful if this is the original one. We may assume that *Wealdstone* means 'the boundary stone in the forest'. The growth of this place dates from the opening of the London & Birmingham railway.

The station was opened by the London & Birmingham Railway as Harrow on 20 July 1837. It was renamed Harrow & Wealdstone on 1 May 1897 and first used by Underground trains on 16 April 1917.

Harrow-on-the-Hill. The history of *Harrow* reminds us of the long ago times before Christianity ousted paganism from England, for the name is derived from the Old English *hearg*, 'heathen temple or shrine'. *Harrow* is a prominent isolated hill rising about 300

feet above the Middlesex plain and here, perhaps on
the site of the present church, must have stood a temple
(or idol) of ancient heathen worship. It was recorded
as *Hergas* in 832 and as *Herges* in Domesday Book
but had changed to *Harowe* by 1369. There is an earlier
name referring to *Gumeninga*; this may be a tribal
people who were pagans—but nothing is really known.
Harrow is famous for its public school.

The station was opened as Harrow on 2 August
1880, and renamed Harrow-on-the-Hill on 1 June 1894.

Hatch End was recorded as *le Haechehend* in 1448 and
is derived from the Old English *haece*, 'a gate, wicket'
and this may have referred to a gate of Pinner Park.
End has the meaning of a quarter-district of a parish.
Therefore *Hatch End* means 'the gate at the end of the
parish'. The name can also be associated with the 14th
century local family of *Hacche*.

The station was opened by the London & Birmingham Railway in 1844 as Pinner. It was renamed Pinner
& Hatch End on 1 January 1897; first used by Underground trains on 16 April 1917, and renamed Hatch
End on 1 February 1920.

Hatton Cross was recorded as *Hatone* in 1230 and is
derived from the Old English *haep*, 'heath' and *tun*, 'a
farm'—and means 'the farm on the heath'. The cross
may have some reference to an old boundary mark, but
more convincingly a reference to the road junction.

The station was opened on 19 July 1975.

Headstone Lane was recorded as *Hegeton* in 1348 and
the origin is in some doubt. It could be a personal name
and the Old English *tun*, 'a farm', but there is no
evidence of this. There was a manor here in the late
12th century belonging to the Archbishop of Canter-
bury. The suggestion that the *stone* is a boundary mark
can only be guessed at, and *Headstone* was not recorded
until 1819.

The station was opened by the London & North

Western Railway on 10 February 1913 and first used by Underground trains on 16 April 1917.

Heathrow Central was recorded as *Hetherewe* in 1547 and was, perhaps, the home of John atte *Hethe* who lived here in the 14th century. The name is derived from (1) the Old English *haep*, 'heath' and *raew*, 'row' —means 'the row of houses on the heath'. This probably referred to some property, maybe owned by John atte Hethe on the western edge of Hounslow Heath or (2) the old English word *ruh* which means 'rough or uncultivated ground', and perhaps Heathrow originally was 'the rough heath'. It now houses one of the world's busiest airports.

The Station was opened 16 December 1977.

Hendon Central was recorded as *Hendun c.* 959 and as *Handone* in Domesday Book. The name is derived from the Old English *haeh*, 'high' and *dun*, 'down or hill'—and means 'At the high hill', referring to the old village of *Hendon* clustered round the church of St. Mary, atop a high hill.

The station was opened on 19 November 1923.

High Barnet was recorded as *la Bernet* in 1235 and is derived from the Old English *baernet*—means 'a place cleared by burning'. *High* refers to its geographical location. Ground was cleared this way by early settlers.

The station was opened by the Great Northern Railway on 1 April 1872 and first used by Underground trains on 14 April 1940.

Highbury & Islington. Originally *Highbury,* was a summer camp of the Romans and during the 13th century the Priory of St. John of Jerusalem had a manor here that was destroyed in 1381. Recorded as *Heybury* during the 14th century, the name is derived from *high* and the Old English *burh,* 'a manor'— means 'the manor on high ground', as opposed to

nearby Canonbury and Barnsbury which stand on
lower ground. *Islington,* recorded as *Gislandune
c.* 1000 and *Isendone* in Domesday Book, is derived
from (1) the personal name *Gisla* and Old English
dun, 'hill or down'—means 'Gisla's hill' referring
to a Saxon and his family who once lived on a site
here, although *Gisla* could be a nickname, (2) the
Old English *Gisel,* 'a hostage' and *dun,* 'hill'—indicating that hostages were once held here or (3) Old English *Isel,* 'lower' and *don*—and can be interpreted as
meaning 'a fortified enclosure'. It was recorded as
Islyndon in 1554.

The station was opened as Highbury on 28 June
1904 and renamed Highbury & Islington on 20 July
1922.

Highgate. From very early times tolls were collected
from travellers who used the Bishop of London's road
across his park at Hornsey which then led to Finchley.
This was at the *High Gate* (*Le Heghgate* recorded in
1354) which gave its name to the hamlet and later
village at one of the highest points in London.

The station was opened by the Great Northern
Railway in 1872, and first used by Underground trains
on 19 January 1941.

(see also **Archway.**)

High Street Kensington. For centuries two roads,
both Roman in origin, one following the lines of the
High Street, were the only means of east-west
communication in this part of London. The first
building in the vicinity took place during the reign
of Charles II (1660–85) to the south of the present
street, while the north side was built up during the
1780s. More development took place in the early
19th century, followed shortly afterwards by the
arrival of the famous shops of the street.

The station was opened on 1 October 1868.

(see also **Kensington Olympia.**)

Hillingdon was recorded as *Hildendun* in 1078 and the
name is derived from the personal name *Hilda* and the

Old English *dun,* 'a hill'—and thus means 'Hilda's Hill' referring to a Saxon and her (or his—for Hilda may be a pet-name for *Hildwalf*) family who once lived here. It was recorded as *Hilendon* in 1254.

The station was opened on 10 December 1923.

Holborn (Kingsway) was recorded as *Holeburne* in 951 and takes its name from part of the River Fleet. It is derived from the Old English *holh,* 'a hollow' and *burna,* 'a stream'—means 'the stream (or brook) in the hollow'. The *hollow* is the valley now spanned by Holborn Viaduct. *Kingsway* is the street that runs from Holborn station to the Aldwych, and was begun in 1901 to clear the slums of this area. It was opened by Edward VII in 1905. There was some controversy over the choice of name but finally *Kingsway* was chosen, no doubt for patriotic reasons.

The station was opened on 15 December 1906 for the Piccadilly Line. The Central Line platforms (replacing British Museum Station) were opened on 25 September 1933.

Holland Park. In the park is *Holland House,* a historic Jacobean mansion begun in 1605 and attributed to John Thorpe, which was originally called Cope's Castle as it was built for Sir Walter Cope. The House passed by marriage to Sir Henry Rich, who was created Earl of *Holland* in Lincolnshire in 1624, and who gave his name to the house and park. The whole estate was sold to the London County Council in 1952.

The station was opened on 30 July 1900.

Holloway Road is a common road name and as it may suggest means 'the way in the hollow'; the road name later became the name of the district. The *hollow* refers to the fact that the hamlets of this area were situated on rather low-lying ground between Highgate and Islington; called *le Holeweye* in 1307.

The station was opened on 15 December 1906.

Hornchurch. From ancient records there is a reference
(in 1222) to the *horned church* (or monastery) in this
district. Nothing of the monks' first church survives
today, but the present building contains a bull's head
and *horns* affixed to the east end, which has been here
since at least 1610. The reason for this is rather
obscure. It is possible that it could be a reference to a
seal of a French monastery or that it could be a
reference to the tanning industry which once flourished
in this area. The present church is St. Andrew's *Hornchurch* and can be found at the far end of the town
situated in the Upminster Road.

The station was opened by the London, Tilbury &
Southend Railway on 1 May 1885, and was first used
by Underground trains on 2 June 1902.

Hounslow Central was recorded as *Honeslaw* in the
Domesday Book and is derived from the Old English
personal name *Hund* and *hlaw,* 'a hill'—means 'the hill
where Hund lived'. It has no connection with dogs
(unlike Houndsditch) as the name may suggest. It was
recorded as *Hounslawe* in 1252.

The station was opened as Heston Hounslow on 1
April 1886; second station opened 19 October 1912;
renamed Hounslow Central 1 December 1925.

Hounslow East—see Hounslow Central.
The first station (on a spur line) was opened on 1
May 1883 as Hounslow; renamed Hounslow Town in
1884. It was closed on 31 March 1886; reopened on 1
March 1903; and finally closed on 1 May 1909. A new
station (on the main line) was opened on 2 May 1909
and renamed Hounslow East 1 December 1925.

Hounslow West—see Hounslow Central.
The station was opened as Hounslow Barracks 21
July 1884; renamed Hounslow West 1 December 1925;
new station opened 11 December 1926.

Hyde Park Corner. A name that occurs frequently both in Domesday Book and in place-names is *hide,* which has been described as 'a piece of ground sufficiently large and fertile to maintain an ordinary household'. *Hyde Park* was named after a hide of land belonging to the Manor of Ebury, for at about the time of Domesday Book the manor was divided into three smaller parts, one being called *Hyde.* From the time of the Norman Conquest until the Dissolution (1066–1536) the Hyde was in the possession of Westminster Abbey. It was then taken by Henry VIII and converted into a royal deer-park. In 1635 Charles I opened it to the public. The *Corner* was the entrance to London until 1825 when the turnpike was removed. It now consists of an open triangular space, enlarged in 1888 when a portion of nearby Green Park was taken for the roadway.

The station was opened on 15 December 1906.

Wellington Arch (Hyde Park Corner)

I

Ickenham was recorded as *Ticheha* in Domesday Book and is derived from the personal name of the Saxon *Ticea* (or *Ica*) and Old English *ham*, 'a home'—and means 'the home of Ica' and his family that once lived on a site here. Recorded as *Ikenham* in 1236.

The station was opened as Ickenham Halt 25 September 1905.

St. James's Palace (Green Park)

Kennington was recorded as *Chenintune* in Domesday Book and is derived from the personal name of the Saxon *Cena* and Old English *tun*, 'a farm'—therefore it means 'the farm of *Cena*' an early inhabitant of the area. It was recorded as *Kenigton* in 1275.

The station was opened on 18 December 1890; closed on 31 May 1923; reconstructed station opened 6 July 1925.

Kensal Green was recorded as *Kingisholte* in 1255 and means the *King's Wood* (*King* and Old English *holt*, 'a wood') but just who the royal owner was is unknown. *The Green* is recorded in 1550 and lies just south of the station; it includes the Kensal Green Cemetery.

The station was opened on 1 October 1916.

Kensington (Olympia) is recorded as *Cheninton* in Domesday Book and the name is derived from the personal name of the Saxon *Cynesige* and the Old English *tun*, 'a farm'—it means 'the farm of Cynesige', another local agriculturist. Has had many variant spellings, with *Kenesingeton* recorded in 1274. *Olympia* is the name of the huge exhibition building opened in 1886 and extended to the main road in 1930.

The station was opened by the West London Railway as Kensington on 27 May 1844; resited farther north 2 June 1862; renamed Kensington (Addison Road) in 1868; renamed Kensington (Olympia) 19 December 1946. First used by Underground trains 1 July 1864.

Kentish Town stands recorded as *Kentisston* in 1208 and the name seems to be derived from a farm held by someone nicknamed *le Kentiss(h)*—and means *Kentish*

Farm, but the real history of the name is, however, unknown. It was only coincidence that Charles Pratt, Earl Camden, obtained through his marriage the Manor of Kentish Town in 1791. He in fact took his name from Camden Place in Kent. The *Town* developed in the later part of the 18th century as an industrialized area of north west London.

The station was opened on 22 June 1907.

Kenton recorded as *Keninton* in 1232 and the name is derived from the personal name of the Saxon *Coena* and the Old English *tun,* 'a farm'—and means 'the farm of Coena' and his family who once lived on a site here (see the similarity with Kennington).

The station was opened by the London & North Western Railway on 15 June 1912 and first used by Underground trains on 16 April 1917.

Kew Gardens, officially the Royal Botanic Gardens, were founded in 1759 by Princess Augusta (mother of George III), in the grounds of Kew House and Richmond Lodge. Kew House was demolished in 1802. Noted for its great variety of plants and wild-life, the gardens now cover 288 acres and were given to the nation by Queen Victoria in 1841. *Kew* is the name of this district on the south bank of the Thames and its name is derived from the Middle English *Key*—meaning 'a quay or wharf'.

The station was opened by the London & South Western Railway on 1 January 1869 and first used by Underground trains on 1 June 1877.

Kilburn, recorded as *Cuneburna* in 1121, takes its name from a stream which rose in Hampstead and flowed across West London, finally joining the River Thames near Chelsea Bridge. Only parts of the stream are in existence today and it has other names in different localities. Where it once turned south to Kilburn High Road it was known as the *Kylbourne* (1502). The name is derived from (1) the Old English *cyne-burna*, 'royal stream' or 'cows' stream', or (2) from a personal name *Cylla* (a once local inhabitant of the area), but the first definition seems correct.

The station was opened as Kilburn & Brondesbury on 24 November 1879; renamed Kilburn on 25 September 1950.

Kilburn Park—see Kilburn.

The only remaining link with the *Park* today is the Kilburn Park Road to the south of the station.

The station was opened on 31 January 1915.

Millbank (Pimlico)

Kingsbury was recorded as *Kynges byrig* in 1046 and as *Chingesberie* in Domesday Book. The name is derived from *Kings*, and the Old English *burh*, 'a fortified place'—and means the 'King's manor or stronghold'. The manor was granted to Westminster Abbey by Edward the Confessor (reigned 1042–66) and the association of the area with a King goes back to at least 957, when the woodland in the parish was referred to as *Kings Wood*. It has had various spellings, being known as *Kynges-bury* in 1199.

The station was opened on 10 December 1932.

King's Cross St. Pancras. The district of North London
now known as *King's Cross* was originally called
Battlebridge, traditionally the site of one of the battles
between Boudicca (Boadicea), the British Queen of
the Iceni, and the Romans about A.D. 59 or 61 at the
bridge over the River Fleet. A corruption in the
Cockney dialect of Bradeford ('broad ford'—over
the Holborn or Fleet River) was recorded in 1207.
Later, however, the district took its present name from a
statue of King George IV which stood from 1830–45 at
crossroads here and this name was generally used when
the then Great Northern Railway adopted the name for
its terminus in 1852, which was constructed on the site
of an old pleasure garden and hospital. *St. Pancras* was
once a solitary village and later a manor granted by
Ethelbert (reigned 860–866) to St. Paul's Cathedral.
Recorded as *Sanctum Pancratiū* in Domesday Book,
the old village took its name from the church dedicated
to the boy martyr *St. Pancras (Pancratius).* According
to tradition this site is one of the first near London on
which a church was built, but now the old church (much
restored) lies nearly forgotten behind the Midland
Railway main-line station named after it, which was
opened in 1868. Tradition has it that the station is
situated on part of Caesar's camp dating from *c.* B.C.
50.

The Metropolitan Line station was opened on 10
January 1863 as King's Cross; renamed King's Cross
& St. Pancras, 1925; King's Cross for St. Pancras,
1927; and King's Cross St. Pancras, 1933. It was
replaced by a new station farther west on 14 March
1941; this new station was adjacent to the tube
stations for the Piccadilly Line (which was opened
on 15 December 1906) and the Northern Line (opened
on 12 May 1907). The building of the Victoria Line
involved extensive reconstruction, and the present
station was finally brought into use on 1 December
1968.

Knightsbridge was recorded as *Cnihtebricge* in 1046 and can be interpreted as meaning 'the bridge of the young men'. It appears that these men were responsible for the upkeep or the defence of the bridge over the Westbourne stream where it crossed the Great West Road. Has had many variant spellings until known as *Knyghtesbrugg* 1364. One story has it that this was the place where knights had their jousting tournaments in days gone by, but this should be taken with that often used 'pinch of salt'. The stream still flows under Albert Gate, Knightsbridge, but is now buried deep in a sewer pipe.

The station was opened on 15 December 1906.

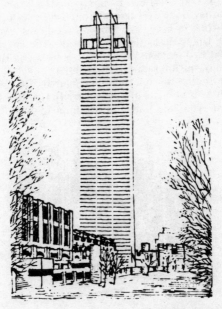

Knightsbridge Barracks (Knightsbridge)

L

Ladbroke Grove. Richard *Ladbrooke* owned the land here in 1624 and his family sold it for building purposes in 1845, giving their name to this long street running to the north of the station.

The station was opened as Notting Hill on 13 June 1864; renamed Notting Hill & Ladbroke Grove 1880; renamed Ladbroke Grove (North Kensington) on 1 June 1919; and Ladbroke Grove in 1938.

Lambeth North. The name *Lambeth* is a reminder of the days when ships from all parts of the world sailed into the heart of London along the River Thames. Recorded in 1041 as *Lambhyo* and as *Lanchei* in Domesday Book, it is derived from Old English *Lambe* and *hythe,* 'a haven' or 'port'—and means 'the port where lambs or cattle are shipped'. The suggestion that the first element of the name is from Old English *lam* 'dirt' or 'mud' can be discounted.

The station was opened as Kennington Road on 10 March 1906; renamed Westminster Bridge Road on 5 August 1906; and Lambeth North on 15 April 1917.

Lambeth Palace (Lambeth North)

Lancaster Gate is one of the gates into Hyde Park and could have received its name in honour of Queen Victoria, in her capacity as Duchess of Lancaster. A street of the same name, roughly opposite the gate, was built in 1863–66.

The station was opened on 30 July 1900.

Latimer Road. Edward *Latymer,* who died in 1626, bequeathed the land either side of the road to support the scholars of Latymer school in which he took an interest. The road runs north to south just west of the station.

The station was opened on 16 December 1868.

Leicester Square. In 1631 Robert Sidney, second Earl of *Leicester,* later British Ambassador to France (1636–41), obtained a licence to build his London residence here at a place then known as *Lammas Land.* The square, which takes its name from the Earl, was laid out in 1665, being called *Leicester Fields* and later *Square,* being converted to a public garden in 1874. *Leicester House* was built on the north side in 1637, pulled down in 1790, rebuilt in the early 19th century and was destroyed by fire in 1865.

The station was opened on 15 December 1906.

Leyton was recorded as *Lugetune c.* 1050 and *Leyton* in 1226. It is derived from *Lea* (the river) and the Old English *tun,* 'a farm'—and thus means 'the farm on the River Lea'. *Lea* is a Celtic name possibly meaning 'light river' or 'sparkling stream'.

The station was opened as Low Leyton by the Eastern Counties Railway on 22 August 1856; renamed Leyton on 1 January 1868. First used by Underground trains on 5 May 1947.

Leytonstone has the same meaning as Leyton with the addition of the word ending, *stone.* Recorded as *Leyton at(te) Stone* in 1370, tradition explains that this spot is near Leyton and the High *Stone,* a boundary mark.

The station was opened by the Eastern Counties Railway on 22 August 1856 and was first used by Underground trains on 5 May 1947.

Liverpool Street. In 1246, on the site now occupied by the station, a priory was erected (later to become the *Bethlehem Hospital)* which stood here until 1676 when it was removed to London Wall. In 1829 the street was widened and named in honour of Lord *Liverpool,* who was Prime Minister from 1812–1827. The whole area was cleared after 1864 for the building and opening for local traffic of the *Liverpool Street* main-line station of the Great Eastern Railway in 1874. Metropolitan Line trains ran into it from 1 February 1875.

The Underground station was opened as Bishopsgate on 12 July 1875 and was renamed Liverpool Street on 1 November 1909.

London Bridge. It is possible that there was a bridge not far east of the present one in the year 43 and there have been many bridges across the River Thames here in the course of history, the fifth and latest one being constructed at a cost of four million pounds and opened in March 1973 and the old bridge being sold and re-erected stone by stone in Arizona. The poem which opens—'London Bridge is broken down' refers to the Battle in 1014 between King Aethelred of the English and the Danes, after which the bridge collapsed. *London* recorded as Londinium *c.* 115 is a Celtic place-name probably formed from a personal name *Londinos*—meaning 'the bold one'.

The Underground station was opened on 25 February 1900.

Loughton, recorded as *Lukintone* in 1062 and as *Lochetuna* in the Domesday Book, is derived from the personal name of the Saxon *Luhha* (or *Luea)* and Old English *tun,* 'a farm'—it means 'the farm of Luhha', an early local Essex inhabitant.

The original station was opened by the Eastern Counties Railway on 22 August 1856. It was resited on 24 April 1865. A new station was opened on 28 April 1940 in readiness for Underground trains, but was first used by Underground trains on 21 November 1948.

Law Courts (Temple)

Maida Vale, although used as the name of a district, is really only a street name. It takes its name from *Maida,* a town in Calabria, Italy, where Sir John Stuart defeated the French in 1806. The street was mentioned in 1868, runs north to south and is, in fact, part of the Edgware Road.

The station was opened on 6 June 1915.

Manor House. Close by the station stands the *Manor House* public house. Known as the 'Manor Tavern' when it was built in *c.* 1820 as a stopping place for travellers between London and Cambridge, it was renamed in 1931 after a *manor house* situated opposite when the public house was rebuilt and the house demolished to make way for St. Olave's Church.

The station was opened on 19 September 1932.

Mansion House has been the official residence of the Lord Mayor of London since 1753. The house was designed by George Dance and built in 1739–53 on the site of the old Stocks market, and St. Mary Wool-church. The building received some damage in the second World War. The City Police Court is in the same building.

The station, which was erected on the site of the Church of Holy Trinity the Less and later a Lutheran church, was opened on 3 July 1871.

Marble Arch was designed by Nash more or less after the 'Arch of Constantine' in Rome and the building was originally erected in 1828 in front of Buckingham Palace. It was removed in 1850–51 to its present site where it was an entrance to Hyde Park until 1908. The arch is constructed of Carrara *marble,* and is described more fully in London Transport's 'Visitor's London'.

See the back of this book for details.

The station was opened on 30 July 1900.

Marble Arch

Marylebone. Local feeling with regard to place names should always be taken into consideration, for there is a story regarding how *Marylebone* received its name. For countless years the place has been known as *Tyburn* (*Tiburne* in Domesday Book) but the association with the tragic tree became too grim and so the local folk took a new name for their parish, being a dedication of the local Church of *St. Mary-on-the-Bourn*, thus 'Tyburn' became *Maryburne* and is recorded in 1453. The *le* (by or near) was added later, the district being known as *Mary le bone* in 1746. Probably the *le* was introduced to sound like St. Mary le Bow. Tyburn survived until the end of the 18th century with the *Tyburn Tree*, an execution place, near the present Marble Arch.

The station was opened as Great Central (from the main line station above) on 27 March 1907; renamed Marylebone 15 April 1917.

Mile End was recorded as *La Mile ende* in 1288. The then hamlet was so named because of its position on the old London–Colchester road at a distance of about *one mile* from Aldgate.

The station was opened on 2 June 1902. Rebuilt and reopened 4 December 1946.

Mill Hill East was recorded as *Myllehill* in 1547 and as the name suggests means 'the mill on the hill'. The original site, *Mill Field*, lies to the north of the present *Mill Hill* village but there is no evidence that a mill ever existed.

The station was opened by the Great Northern Railway on 22 August 1867 as Mill Hill; renamed Mill Hill East on 1 March 1928. First used by Underground trains on 18 May 1941 mainly to serve the nearby barracks.

Mansion House

Monument. This well-known London landmark was erected during the 1670s and is a hollow column 202 feet high designed by Sir Christopher Wren and Robert Hooke. It commemorates the Great Fire of London in 1666 and the height of the monument is said to be the exact distance from the baker's shop in nearby Pudding Lane where the fire started.

The station was opened as Eastcheap on 6 October 1884 and renamed Monument on 1 November 1884. The Bank-Monument subway was opened on 18 September 1933.

Moorgate. As the name suggests this was the site of one of the *gates* in the old City wall. The first *Moor gate* was cut into the wall in 1415 to give access to the moorland lying to the north of London. As the wall crumbled during the 18th century the gate was demolished in 1760. The thoroughfare called *Moorgate* was built in 1846 and, in fact, runs from the site of the old gate.

The station was opened as Moorgate Street on 23 December 1865 and renamed Moorgate on 24 October 1924. The Northern Line station, always called Moorgate, was opened on 25 February 1900.

Moor Park was recorded as *la More c.* 1180 and the meaning is self-explanatory. The original site of the settlement was evidently a *Moor Farm* which once stood in the River Colne water meadows, near a tract of marshy land.

The station was opened as Sandy Lodge on 9 May 1910; renamed Moor Park & Sandy Lodge on 18 October 1923 and Moor Park on 25 September 1950.

Morden was recorded as *Mordone* in Domesday Book and the name is derived from Old English *mor,* 'a marsh' and *dun,* 'a hill'—it means 'marshy hill' but the interpretation 'hill in the fens' seems more correct. *Morden* occupies a hill overlooking lower ground.

The station was opened on 13 September 1926.

Monument

Mornington Crescent was begun in 1821 by Ferdinand, the second Lord Southampton, and is named after a famous connection of the family. For the Lord's sister-in-law was Anne Wellesley, whose maiden name was *Mornington*, being the daughter of the Earl of Mornington and sister of the Duke of Wellington.

The station was opened on 22 June 1907.

N

Neasden was recorded as *Neasdun* in 939 and the name is derived from the Old English *naess*, 'nose' and *dun*, 'hill'—it means 'the nose-shaped hill' referring to a well defined landmark of this area. Known as *Needsden* in 1750, and the present spelling appeared at a later date.

The station was opened on 2 August 1880 as Kingsbury & Neasden; renamed Neasden & Kingsbury on 1 January 1910 and Neasden on 1 January 1932.

Newbury Park was recorded in 1348 and is derived from *new* and Old English *burh*, 'manor house'— means 'the (then) new manor', in the *park*.

The station was opened by the Great Eastern Railway on 1 May 1903 and was first used by Underground trains on 14 December 1947.

New Cross. It is recorded that in the 15th century *New Cross Heath* was situated here and, during the second Civil War in 1648, a skirmish took place nearby. The name is derived from the *cross* roads where the east-west road passed through Camberwell, cutting the road from Kent and the south. Later at this junction stood an old coaching tavern, the 'Golden Cross'.

The station was opened for East London Line trains on 1 April 1880.

New Cross Gate—see New Cross.
The *Gate* stood at the junction of Queens Road and New Cross Road, and was taken down on 31 October 1865 by the Metropolitan Board of Works.

The station was opened as New Cross for East London Line trains on 7 December 1869; it was renamed New Cross Gate on 9 July 1923.

North Acton—see Acton Town.

The station was opened on 5 November 1923. (There had been a Great Western Railway halt named North Acton, to the west of the present station, from 2 May 1904 to 31 January 1913).

North Ealing—see Ealing Broadway.

The station was opened on 23 June 1903.

Northfields is a new district name preserving the old field-name *Northfield* which is self-explanatory, being recorded in 1455.

The station was opened as Northfield Halt on 16 April 1908; renamed Northfields & Little Ealing 11 December 1911; resited as Northfields, east of the old site, on 19 May 1932.

North Harrow—see Harrow-on-the-Hill.

The station was opened on 22 March 1915.

Northolt was recorded as *nord healum* in 960 and as *Northala* in Domesday Book and the name is derived from the Old English *nord,* 'north' and *health,* 'heath'—it means 'the north heath' or 'angle of land'. The *north* being in contrast to Southall. Known as *Northolt* by 1610.

The station was opened for Underground trains on 21 November 1948. It replaced a halt named Northolt which had been opened by the Great Western Railway on 1 May 1907.

North Weald takes its name from a natural location of this part of Essex and is derived from the Old English *wald* (or *weald*), 'forest' or 'woodland'—especially referring to high forest land—it means simply 'the north wood'.

The station was opened by the Great Eastern Railway on 24 April 1865; first used by Underground trains on 18 November 1957.

Royal Festival Hall (Waterloo)

North Wembley—see Wembley Central.
The station was opened by the London & North
Western Railway on 15 June 1912, and was first used
by Underground trains on 16 April 1917.

Northwick Park is a modern name and comes from the
Northwick family, Lords of the Manor of Harrow in
1797.
  The station was opened as Northwick Park & Kenton
on 28 June 1923; renamed Northwick Park, 15 March
1937.

Northwood was recorded as *Northwode* in 1435 and
was originally the name of a *Wood* and farm lying to
the *north* of Ruislip. The present town dates chiefly
from the construction of the railway *c.* 1885.
  The station was opened on 1 September 1887.

Northwood Hills—see Northwood.

The *Hills* refer to nearby high ground. The station may have received its name as a result of a public competition sponsored by the Metropolitan Railway.

The station was opened on 13 November 1933.

Notting Hill Gate was recorded as *Knottynghull* in 1356 but the origin of the name is in some doubt. It may be taken from (1) the Old English *cnotting*, 'a hill' or (2) more probably it is the name (or nickname) for a family who settled in this area in early times, called *Knotting*. Recorded as *Noding Hill* in 1680 and with the present spelling at a later date. (The district was for some time known as the Gravel Pits (1654); once this referred to the area near the *gate*, which formerly stood here at the junction of Kensington Church Street and the main road and was removed in 1864.)

The station was opened on 1 October 1868; the reconstructed station was opened on 1 March 1959 and completed on 31 July 1960.

Osterley House (Osterley)

Oakwood takes its name from the nearby *Oakwood Park,* or possibly a large house which once stood here called *Oak Lodge.*

The station was opened as Enfield West on 13 March 1933; renamed Enfield West (Oakwood) 3 May 1934, and Oakwood 1 September 1946.

Old Street was recorded as *Ealdestrate c.* 1200 and *le Oldestrete* in 1373. Originally a Roman Road, then the old highway from the Alders-gate to the north-east of England, before Bishopsgate was built.

The station was opened on 17 November 1901.

Ongar was recorded as *Aungre* in the 11th century and refers to a nearby natural feature as the name is derived from the Old English *angr*—meaning simply 'grazing land'. Changed to *Ongar* in the course of time.

The station was opened by the Great Eastern Railway on 24 April 1865 and first used by Underground trains on 18 November 1957.

Osterley was recorded as *Osterle* in 1274 and the name is derived from either (1) the Old English word *eowestre,* which can be interpreted as meaning—'sheepfold clearing', being once pasture land, or (2) Old English *ost,* 'a knob of land' and *leah*, 'a glade', which can be interpreted as meaning 'a hillock'. Recorded as *Austerley* 1609 and *Osterley* at a later date.

The station was opened as Osterley & Spring Grove on 1 May 1883. It was resited further west and the new station opened on 25 March 1934 as Osterley. The earlier station can still be seen.

Oval is the famous ground of the Surrey County Cricket Club which was formed in 1884, the name *Oval* coming from the shape of the ground. The first piece of turf was laid in March 1845. The first cricket match was played on or about 13 May of that year, and the first Test match in England (v. Australia) in 1880.

The station was opened on 18 December 1890.

Oxford Circus takes its name from *Oxford Street* of which it forms a part. This was the old road to *Oxford* in 1682, Oxford Road in 1720, and Oxford Street in 1725. The *Circus* was originally named Regent Circus, as it is at the intersection with Regent Street.

The station was opened on 30 July 1900.

London's Costers (Lambeth North)

Paddington was recorded as *Padintune* in 959 and the name is derived from the personal name of the Saxon *Padda* and the Old English *tun*, 'a farm'—it means 'the farm of Padda', a local inhabitant. Recorded as *Patyngton* in 1398 and changed to *Paddington* in the course of time.

The station was opened as Paddington (Praed Street) 1 October 1868; renamed Paddington 11 July 1948. The Bakerloo Line station was opened on 1 December 1913.

Park Royal was the grand name given to a piece of land where an unsuccessful attempt was made to establish a fixed ground for the Royal Agricultural Society Annual Show. Before the first World War the land was built over and the name became that of a district.

The station was opened as Park Royal & Twyford Abbey on 23 June 1903; resited 6 July 1931 and renamed Park Royal.

Parsons Green. As the name suggests, this was the hamlet which grew up round the *parsonage* house of Fulham, being recorded as *Personesgrene* in 1391. The *Green* is now a small triangular piece of land on the edge of which stands the parish church.

The station was opened on 1 March 1880.

Perivale. This district was originally known as Greneford and is recorded as this in Domesday Book, later to be known as Little Greenford (in 1386) being a distinction from Greenford (or Great Greenford). The name was changed by 1508 to *Pyryvale* and is derived from Middle English *perie*, 'pear tree' and Old French *val*, 'vale'—and means 'the valley with the pear trees', which referred to a nearby

meadow. Called *Purevale* in the late 16th century, it
changed to the present spelling in the course of time.

The station was opened for Underground trains on
30 June 1947. It replaced a Perivale halt on the Great
Western Railway opened on 2 May 1904.

Piccadilly Circus. The name *Piccadilly* is probably
derived from *Pickadilly Hall,* the popular name of a
house built in *c.* 1611 near Windmill Street by a retired
tailor, Robert Baker, who made much of his fortune by
the sale of 'pickadillies', a form of collar or ruff. The
street was known as *Portugal Street* in 1692 in honour
of Catharine of Braganza, the Queen of Charles II, but
changed to *Pickadilly Street* by 1763. *The Circus,* built
during the 19th century, covers the site of a house and
garden belonging to a Lady Hutton; the garden was
near a field known as the Round Ringill.

The station was opened on 10 March 1906. The
rebuilt and extensively reconstructed station was
opened on 10 December 1928.

Pimlico is a comparatively new district of London,
recorded as *Pimplico* in 1630 and mention is made of
the Kings highway at *Pimplico* referring to the road to
Chelsea in 1681. It seems that the name was copied
from a garden of public entertainment in Hoxton (north
London), named after its owner, a well known
inn-keeper—Ben *Pimlico,* whose name was also given
to his inn (late 16th-century). There was once a *Pimlico
Walk* in Hoxton. *Pimlico* on the north bank of the
River Thames, was almost uninhabited before the 19th
century.

The station was opened on 14 September 1972.

Pinner was recorded as *Pinnora* in 1232 and the name
is derived from a personal name (or nickname) *Pin* (or
Pinna), and the Old English *ora,* 'bank edge' or
'slope'—this refers to the original village street which
slopes steeply up to the church from the Pinn
River—and thus means 'the slope to Pinna's place'. It

is certain that the River *Pinn* takes its name from the old village and not vice versa. It was recorded as *Pynnor* in 1483.

The station was opened on 25 May 1885.

Piccadilly Circus

Plaistow was recorded as *Plagestoue c.* 1200 and was the ancient site of a Manor and a place of court meetings. It was also, on occasions, the place where 'miracle plays' and similar entertainments were performed. The name is derived from the Old English *pleg,* 'sports' or 'playing' and *stowe,* 'place'—and means, simply, 'the playing-place'.

The station was opened by the London, Tilbury & Southend Railway on 31 March 1858; first used by Underground trains on 2 June 1902.

Preston Road was mentioned as *Preston* in 1194 and the name comes from the Old English *preast,* 'priest' and *tun* 'farm'—and means 'the farm belonging to the priest(s)'. A priest is mentioned in Domesday Book, as holding land in the parish of Harrow, possibly at this location. The *road* was added to the name as the district grew in the course of time.

The station was opened as a halt on 21 May 1908; new station (resited) 22 November 1931.

Putney Bridge was recorded as *Putelei* in the Domesday Book and the name is derived from the Saxon personal name *Puttan* and Old English *hyp*, 'a landing place'—means 'Puttan's wharf'. This was one of many such landing places on the River Thames. The original wooden *bridge* was erected in 1729 and replaced by the present stone bridge in 1884–86. It was widened in 1933.

The station was opened on 1 March 1880 as Putney Bridge & Fulham; renamed Putney Bridge & Hurlingham 1 September 1902; Putney Bridge 1932.

Admiralty Arch (Trafalgar Square)

Queensbury really means 'a fortified place' but do not look for the remains in this part of north-west London. When the new Metropolitan Line to Stanmore was opened on 10 December 1932, one station was called Kingsbury. Two years later, a further station was opened and the name *Queensbury* was invented for it. Here then is a case of a district getting its name from a railway station!

The station was opened on 16 December 1934.

Queen's Park was the name adopted for a housing estate by the *park* that was built from the late 1870s onwards. It was so named in honour of Queen Victoria.

The present station replaced the original L. & N.W. Rly. one, opened as Queen's Park (West Kilburn) on 2 June 1879.

The station was opened for Underground trains on 11 February 1915.

Queensway, formerly called Black Line Lane, was named from the Public House once on the corner of the street. Was renamed in honour of *Queen* Victoria soon after she came to the throne in 1837. It is suggested that the reason was that, as a child, this was the place of Victoria's favourite horse ride; she then lived only half a mile away at Kensington Palace. It was called *Queen's Road,* then *Queensway.*

The station was opened as Queen's Road on 30 July 1900; renamed Queensway 1 September 1946.

R

Ravenscourt Park was the manor granted to Alice Perrers, the notorious favourite of Edward III (reigned 1327–77). It was known as Palyngewyk in 1270 (later Padingwick) and in 1819 a *Raven's Court House* was recorded in the area, but the history of this modern name is unknown. *The Park* lies opposite the station along Paddenswick Road.

The station was opened by the London & South Western Railway on 1 April 1873 as Shaftesbury Road. It was renamed Ravenscourt Park on 1 March 1888. First used by Underground trains on 1 June 1877.

Royal Opera Arcade (Covent Garden)

Rayners Lane was developed as a suburban residential area in the 1930s. There is a pretty legend that the name arose from one *Rayner,* an old shepherd who lived in a solitary cottage here, in the early days of the Metropolitan Railway, which opened the station on 26 May 1906 as a halt.

Redbridge takes its name from the *bridge* over the River Roding on what is now the Eastern Avenue just outside Wanstead. The old *red bridge,* first recorded on a map in 1746, was probably a century older; it has been replaced by a more modern one but the original bridge gave its name to a whole new London borough.

The station was opened on 14 December 1947.

Regent's Park, once Marylebone Park, was a Royal Hunting ground until the Interregnum, 1649. It reverted to the Crown in 1811 and was laid out afresh from 1812 onwards by John Nash for the Prince *Regent,* after whom it is named. At the same time Nash designed and built Regent Street as part of the 'Royal Mile' connecting the park with the Prince's house in St. James's. Roughly circular in shape, the Park covers an area of 472 acres and includes the famous London Zoo.

The station was opened on 10 March 1906.

Richmond was known as Shene (meaning Shelter) from *c.* 950 until 1502, when Henry VIII rebuilt the palace here after it had been burnt down by fire a year earlier. He called it *Richmond* (or *Richemount*) after his earldom so named in Yorkshire. This, in its turn, originally came from a name of a place in France. So modern *Richmond,* as we see, has obtained its name in a very roundabout way.

The terminal station was opened by the London & South Western Railway on 1 January 1869 and first used by Underground trains on 1 June 1877. The original London & South Western Railway station was opened on 27 July 1846.

Rickmansworth was recorded as *Prichemareworde* in Domesday Book and the name is derived from a personal name *Ricmaer* and Old English *worp*, 'enclosure'—and means 'Ricmaer's farm with the enclosure'. It seems that *Ricmaer* is a continental name and this person had recently come from Europe and settled here. There have been many changes of spelling including *Rikmersworth* in 1430, until the present spelling was adopted.

The station was opened on 1 September 1887.

Roding Valley takes its name from the River *Roding*. The river, however, took its name from the villages called *Reding* (or *Roothing*), which in turn came from the settlement of the people known as the *Hroda,* and was corrupted to *Roding* in the course of time. Recorded as *duae Rotinges* in the 11th century and as *Rodon* in 1576. *The Valley* as such is no more than a shallow dip at this point.

The station was opened by the London & North Eastern Railway on 3 February 1936 and was first used by Underground trains on 21 November 1948.

Rotherhithe was mentioned as *Aetheredes Hyth* in a charter of 893 and recorded as *Rederhia* in the early 12th century. The name is derived from the Old English *hryder,* 'cattle' and *hyo,* 'hithe' or 'landing place'—and means 'the landing place for cattle', and recalls the time when ships travelled up the River Thames from all over the world. It is suggested that the first part of the name refers to an ancient mariner *Retha,* but this can be discounted. It was recorded as *Rotherheth* in 1268.

The station was opened on 7 December 1869.

Royal Oak was the name of an old rural tavern, the entrance to which was by way of a wooden plank over the Westbourne River. This has now been replaced by the 'Railway Tap' public house which contains much of interest for any railway enthusiast. The station and

district now take their name from the old tavern.
The station was opened on 30 October 1871.

Ruislip was recorded as *Rislepe* in Domesday Book
and the name has one of London's most curious origins
derived from Old English *ryse,* 'rush' and *hlype,* 'leap'.
It seems to refer to a spot where the little River Pinn
could once be crossed. It has had various spellings until
recorded as *Ruislip* in 1527.
The station was opened on 4 July 1904.

Ruislip Gardens—see Ruislip.
The *Gardens* were taken from the name of a nearby
1930s housing development.
The station was opened on 21 November 1948.

Ruislip Manor—see Ruislip.
Today near the River Pinn lies *Manor* farm. This, and
its surroundings, once held a priory dependent on the
Norman Abbey of Bec. During the wars with France
the Manor was confiscated by the Crown and the priory
was closed in 1414. The land was granted to the Earl of
Bedford, then to King's College, Cambridge, who still
own the lordship of the manor.
The station was opened as a halt on 5 August 1912.

Russell Square was named in 1800 by an Act of
Parliament and was built between 1801–05. It takes its
name from the Dukes of Bedford whose family name is
Russell; they acquired lands in London in 1552 and
later by marriage in 1669. The square was once part of
an area known as Southampton Fields and later called
Long Fields. The square was badly damaged during the
second World War, but has been redeveloped since to
become the second largest square in London.
The station was opened on 15 December 1906.

St. James's Park lies on the site of an ancient hospital dedicated to *St. James the Less,* from which it takes its name. It was part of a swamp until, on the orders of Henry VIII in 1532, it was drained to become a bowling alley, tilt yard, and breeding ground for deer. John Nash redesigned the park in 1827–9.

The station was opened on 25 December 1868.

Epstein carving (St. James's Park)

St. John's Wood was recorded *Sci Johannis* in 1294, and the *wood* was granted to the Knights Templars of St. John of Jerusalem but later passed into the possession of the Hospitallers of this Order. This fashionable district of north-west London was first recorded as *(Grete) St. John's Wood* in 1558.

The station was opened as St. John's Wood Road on 13 April 1868; renamed St. John's Wood on 1 April 1925; renamed Lords on 11 June 1939; and replaced by the new St. John's Wood Station on the Bakerloo Line on 20 November 1939 when Lords Station was closed.

St. Paul's takes its name from the nearby Cathedral of the Diocese of London. The tradition that a Roman temple once stood here has no evidence to support it. There was, however, a Christian Church built here in the 7th century which was destroyed by fire in 1087. This is the third Cathedral built on the present site, and was planned by Sir Christopher Wren after the previous one had been destroyed in the Great Fire of London in 1666. Construction commenced in 1675 and was completed some 27 years later.

The station was opened as Post Office on 30 July 1900, and renamed St. Paul's on 1 February 1937; reconstructed station opened 1 January 1939.

Seven Sisters took its name, not from a family of seven sisters, but from *seven* elm trees which stood near Page Green, where the Seven Sisters Road (built 1831–3) joined the old Ermine Street. They were marked as *7 Sesters* in 1754, then *Seven Sisters* in 1805.

The station was opened on 1 September 1968.

Shadwell was recorded as *Scadeuuelle* in Domesday Book and as *Shadewell* in 1233 and means—a 'shallow well' from a once nearby local spring. Once also known as *Chadwell,* it has been suggested to be from a spring dedicated to *St. Chad.*

The station was opened on 10 April 1876.

Shepherd's Bush either takes its name from the *shepherds* who used this place as a meadow or more likely from a personal name of someone so called. Recorded as *Sheppards Bush Green* in 1635, and now called *Shepherd's Bush Common.*

The Central Line station was opened on 30 July 1900, and the Hammersmith & City Line station on 13 June 1864; the latter was resited and new station opened on 1 April 1914.

Shoreditch was originally a village situated on an old Roman highway. Was recorded as *Soredich c.* 1148 and the name means—'the ditch of the bank', literally the *Shore-ditch*. The nature of both the bank and the ditch are unknown, but it could not be the shore of the Thames as sometimes suggested. It did not receive its name from (1) Jane *Shore* or (2) The Lord of the Manor who once lived here, named *Soerditche*—both these suggestions must be attributed to local folk-lore.

The station was opened on 10 April 1876.

St. Paul's

Sloane Square. Like many other street names in this part of London, the square is named in honour of Sir Hans *Sloane* (1660–1753) the physician and botanist who purchased the manor of Chelsea from the Cheyne family in 1712. In 1749 his great collection of books and curiosities formed the basis of the British Museum. Over the station, through a square iron conduit 15 feet above the platforms, passes the River Westbourne which eventually reaches the River Thames by Chelsea Bridge.

The station was opened on 24 December 1868; severely damaged by enemy action on 12 November 1940; rebuilding after the second World War was completed on 3 May 1951.

Snaresbrook was so named in 1599 and takes its name from a nearby natural landmark. The name is derived from the Old English *shear,* 'swift' and *brook*—means 'the swift flowing brook'.

The station was built as Snaresbrook & Wanstead by the Eastern Counties Railway and opened on 22 August 1856. First used by Underground trains and renamed Snaresbrook on 14 December 1947.

South Ealing—see Ealing Broadway.
The station was opened on 1 May 1883.

Southfields was recorded as *Suthfield* in 1247 and takes its name from a great *field* where farm produce was once sold.
The station was opened on 3 June 1889.

Southgate was so recorded in 1370 and was known as *le Southgate* in 1608. The hamlet here grew up at the *south gate* of Enfield Chase and is so named.
The station was opened on 13 March 1933.

South Harrow—see Harrow-on-the-Hill.
The station was opened on 28 June 1903. It was resited on 5 July 1935.

South Kensington—see Kensington.
The station was opened on 24 December 1868, and the Piccadilly Line tube station on 8 January 1907.

South Kenton—see Kenton.
The station was opened on 3 July 1933.

South Ruislip—see Ruislip.
The station was opened on 21 November 1948. The station on the adjacent Western Region line was opened by the Great Western & Great Central Joint Committee as Northolt Junction on 1 May 1908. It was renamed South Ruislip & Northolt Junction on 12 September 1932, and became South Ruislip on 30 June 1947.

Chelsea Pensioner (Sloane Square)

South Wimbledon—see Wimbledon.
The station was opened on 13 September 1926.

South Woodford—see Woodford.
The station was opened as George Lane on 22
August 1856 by the Eastern Counties Railway. It was
renamed South Woodford (George Lane) on 5 July
1937, and South Woodford in 1950. First used by
Underground trains on 14 December 1947.

Stamford Brook was recorded in 1650 and this was the
name of the stream which divided, near its mouth, to
the west, the parishes of Acton and Chiswick from
Fulham, and further north was spanned by Bollo
Bridge. The name is derived from a *stony ford,* once
located here, where the main Great West Road crossed
the stream.
   The station was opened on 1 February 1912.

Stanmore was recorded *Stanmere* in Domesday
Book and the name is derived from the Old English
stan, 'stony' and *mere,* 'a pool'—and means the 'stony
pool'. There are outcrops of gravel on the clay soil here
and the *mere* may have been one of the ponds which
still exist. Known as *Stanmore the Great* in 1574—'the
Great' distinguished it from Whitchurch or Little
Stanmore.
   The station was opened on 10 December 1932.

Stepney Green was recorded as *Stybbanhype c.* 1000 and as *Stibenhede* in Domesday Book and the name is derived from the Saxon personal name *Stebbing* and Old English *hyo,* 'hithe' or 'landing place'—and thus means 'Stybba's landing place', showing that even in Saxon times Stepney was associated with ships and the sea. It has had various spellings in the course of time until recorded as *Stepney* in 1534. *The Green* is now a street and was the home of John atte *Grene,* and so named in 1682.

The station was opened on 23 June 1902.

Stockwell was recorded as *Stokewell* in 1188 and can be interpreted as meaning—'the stream with a footbridge consisting of a tree trunk', referring to a natural location, which was once nearby. Stockwell was a small rural village until the 1860's.

The station was opened on 18 December 1890.

Stonebridge Park. Where the Harrow Road crosses the River Brent stood a *stone bridge,* first recorded in 1745, that now gives its name to the district. It was recorded in 1875 that there was a cluster of 60 or 80 villas on a nearby estate which was given the name *Stonebridge Park.*

The station was opened by the London & North Western Railway on 15 June 1912 and first used by Underground trains on 16 April 1917.

Science Museum (South Kensington)

Stratford was recorded in 1177 and is derived from the Old English *straet,* 'road' and *ford*—and means 'the road with a ford'. The ford was where the Roman road to Colchester crossed one of the various branches of the River Lea.

The station was opened on 4 December 1946. (The original Eastern Counties Railway station was opened on 20 June 1839.)

Sudbury Hill—see Sudbury Town.
The Hill is the high ground to the north of Sudbury.

The station was opened on 28 June 1903.

Sudbury Town was recorded as *Suthbury* in 1282 and the name is derived from *south* and Old English *burh,* 'manor'—and means 'the south manor', for it lies to the south-east of Harrow. The *Town* was built up during the later part of the 19th century.

The station was opened on 28 June 1903.

Surrey Docks were opened in 1807, and were once the centre of the timber trade, but are now closed. The name *Surrey* dates from the settlements of the Saxons on both sides of the River Thames and means—'The Southern Region'.

The station was opened as Deptford Road on 7 December 1869 and was first used by Underground trains on 1 October 1884; renamed Surrey Docks 17 July 1911.

Swiss Cottage takes its name from a famous London public house. Here once stood an old toll gate keeper's cottage, then later a chalet. *The Swiss Tavern* was built in 1803–4, the name being changed to *Swiss Cottage* at a later date. The building was reconstructed in 1965. Built to the design of a Swiss cottage, it claims to be the largest 'pub' in London. When the railway was extended, during the later part of the 19th century, to this part of north-west London the name was taken for the station, and now for the district.

The station was opened on 13 April 1868; the original platforms were closed as from 18 August 1940 and replaced by the new Bakerloo Line station opened on 20 November 1939.

Nelson's Column (Trafalgar Square)

T

Temple. The site of the Law Courts and London's lawyers stands on land once owned by the Knights *Templars,* members of a military and religious Order founded in Jerusalem in about 1118. Their task was to protect the holy places and their name derives from the place where they had their quarters, near the site of Solomon's *Temple.* The name Temple was also given to their quarters in London and Paris. The Pope dissolved the Order in 1312 and the buildings have been used by the legal profession from the 14th century.

The station was opened on 30 May 1870.

Temple Church (Temple)

Theydon Bois. Was known as *Thayden de Bosco* and held by *Hugh de Bossco* in 1240, but this family name seems to be of local and not French origin and is derived from the *wood* in *Theydon. Theydon* itself means, perhaps, a 'valley where thatch was obtained'.

The station was opened as Theydon by the Great Eastern Railway on 24 April 1865; renamed Theydon Bois on 1 December 1865. First used by Underground trains on 25 September 1949.

Tooting Bec was recorded as *Totinge* in 675 and
Totinge in Domesday Book. From *c.* 1082 it
comprised two manors—that of *Upper Tooting* and
Tooting Bec, held in 1086 by the Abbey of St. Mary of
Bec in Normandy and *Tooting Bec* is so named.
Tooting is derived from a personal name of the Saxon
Tota and the Old English place name word ending *ing,*
literally 'the people who lived at'—Tooting, therefore
means—'the home of Tota's people'. It is suggested
that it should be also interpreted as 'people of the
look-out place' but this is doubtful as there is no hill in
Tooting.

The station was opened as Trinity Road on 13
September 1926; renamed Tooting Bec 1 October
1950.

Tooting Broadway—see Tooting.
The *Broadway,* once a large open space, is now a small
triangular area near the station.

The station was opened on 13 September 1926.

Tottenham Court Road was recorded as *Tottenheale*
c. 1000 and is derived from the personal name of
William de *Tottenhall's* land and manor which, at the
time of the Norman Conquest, belonged to the
Deanery of St. Paul's Cathedral. Later called *Toten*
Hall which lay at the north-west corner of the present
road. There was an ancient *court* here, much of which
was demolished in 1765 to make way for the Euston
Road. By the 17th century the place had become a tea
garden and public amusement centre. During the early
19th century the road was built up when Bloomsbury
to the east was being developed, although much was
reconstructed in the early 1900s.

The Central Line station was opened on 30 July
1900; the adjacent Northern Line station was opened
as Oxford Street on 22 June 1907 and renamed
Tottenham Court Road on 9 March 1908 (see also
Goodge Street).

Tottenham Hale. Tottenham was recorded as *Toteham* in Domesday Book and the name is derived from the personal name of the Saxon *Totta* and Old English *ham,* 'a homestead'—and means 'the home of Totta' and his family who once lived on a site here. *Hale* is derived from the Old English *healh,* 'a corner of land'. It was recorded as *le Hale* in 1502 and was the home of Richard atte *Hale* in 1274.

The station was opened on 1 September 1968.

British Museum (Holborn or Tottenham Court Road)

Totteridge & Whetstone. *Totteridge* was recorded as *Taterugg* in 1248 and is derived from the personal name of a Saxon *Totta* and a ridge of a hill where he lived—and thus means 'Totta's ridge'. *Whetstone* was recorded as *Wheston* in 1417 and means 'the stone quarry'. Tradition holds that there was once a large stone here on which the soldiers sharpened their steel before the battle of Barnet in 1471.

The station was opened by the Great Northern Railway as Totteridge on 1 April 1872 and was renamed Totteridge & Whetstone on 1 April 1874. It was first used by Underground trains on 14 April 1940.

Tower Hill was recorded as *Tourhulle* in 1343 and takes its name from the nearby *Tower of London*, notorious in history as the place of public execution of the traitors taken here from the Tower. 125 people are known to have died here between 1381–1745 and a slab in nearby Trinity Square Gardens marks the scaffold site. At the foot of *Tower Hill* stands a new kiosk to that which from 1870–96 was the entrance to London's first tube tunnel under the Thames.

The station was opened as Mark Lane on 6 October 1884 and renamed Tower Hill 1 September 1946. It was resited on 5 February 1967 on the place where a station called Tower of London had been in use from 25 September 1882 to 12 October 1884.

Trafalgar Square was designed by Sir Charles Barry and constructed in 1829–41 and covers the site of The Mews where the royal falconry was situated. It was recorded as this in 1294. The name *Trafalgar* commemorates the naval battle of 1805. Nelson's Column in the square was erected between 1840–43 and the four lions at the foot of the column were added in 1867.

The station was opened on 10 March 1906, and will be renamed Charing Cross as part of the new station complex, combining Trafalgar Square and Strand Stations (see Charing Cross Embankment).

Tufnell Park was named in honour of William *Tufnell* who held the manor of Barnsbury in 1753. *Tufnell Park Road* runs to the east of the station, but there is no park in the area.

The station was opened on 22 June 1907.

Turnham Green was recorded as *Turneham* in *c.* 1229 and was once a hamlet on the Great West Road. The name is derived from the Old English *turn*, 'circular' and *hamm*, 'a water meadow'—and means literally 'the bend at the river' referring to the nearby River Thames. *The Green* was first recorded in 1396 where

Christ Church now stands. Incidentally, it was here, during the Civil War, that King Charles's troops were checked by the rebel Parliament's Trained Bands of Londoners.

The station was opened by the London & South Western Railway on 1 January 1869 and first used by Underground trains on 1 June 1877. The rebuilt station was opened on 3 December 1911.

Turnpike Lane once belonged to the 'Stamford Hill and Green Lanes Turnpike Trust' and a *turnpike* gate was erected in 1767 at the Hornsey *Lane* (now Tottenham Lane) end of the road; it was removed in the 1870s.

The station was opened on 19 September 1932.

Tower Bridge (Tower Hill)

U

Upminster was recorded as *Upmynstre* in 1062 and the name is derived from *mynster,* which refers to a church served by several clergy, rather than to a monastery. The prefix *up* means 'higher ground', although the town does not rise much above sixty feet. *Upminster* means—'the church on high land'. The name of this area was originally Chafford, a corruption of St. Chad's Ford and tradition asks us to believe that the brothers St. Chad and St. Cedd used it as one of their preaching centres when they brought Christianity to Essex in *c.* 670.

The station was opened by the London, Tilbury & Southend Railway on 1 May 1885 and first used by Underground trains on 2 June 1902.

Upminster Bridge—see Upminster.
To the right of the station, under the railway bridge and near the 'Bridge House' pub, there is a small iron road bridge, marked *Upminster Bridge.* Tradition has it that the Romans built a ford here over the River Ingrebourne during Cæsar's invasion of England. It seems that in *c.* 1300 a wooden bridge was built to replace the ford, while the present bridge was erected by the Essex County Council in 1891.

The station was opened on 17 December 1934.

Upney simply means the *upper-stream* and this local natural feature gives the name to this district.

The station was opened on 12 September 1932.

Upton Park. Upton is derived from *up* and Old English *tun*—a farm—and means 'the farm, or homestead on higher ground' once in a *park,* and the district is so named.

The station was opened by the London, Tilbury &

Southend Railway in 1877 and first used by Underground trains on 2 June 1902.

Uxbridge was recorded as *Oxebruge c.* 1145 and the name is derived from a 7th century tribe, the Wixan, who settled here, and in the course of time this has been abbreviated to *Ux*. The *bridge* is an ancient one over the river Colne and has variant spellings until recorded as *Uxbridge* in 1398.

The station was opened on 4 July 1904, which was replaced by a resited station on 4 December 1938.

Vauxhall is named from the Norman *Falkes de Breauté* who obtained the manor of Lambeth by his marriage to the heiress Margaret de Riparus (or Redvers) in *c.* 1220, the manor being granted to him in 1233. Recorded as *Faukeshale* in 1279, corrupted to *Fox Hall* then eventually to *Vauxhall*.

The station was opened on 23 July 1971.

Victoria. Like many other places the station was named in honour of Queen *Victoria*. The main-line station, opened on 1 October 1860, stands on piles over the basin of the former Grosvenor Canal.

The Underground station was opened on 24 December 1868.

Walthamstow Central was recorded as *Wilcumestowe* c. 1075 and the name is derived from (1) the Old English *wilcume*, 'welcome' and *stow*, 'a holy place', and therefore means—'the holy place with a welcome' or (2) a religious place once founded here by a woman named *Wilcume*. It was recorded as *Walthanstowe* in 1446.

The original station was opened by the Great Eastern Railway as Walthamstow (Hoe Street) on 26 April 1870; it was renamed Walthamstow Central on 6 May 1968. Underground trains ran from 1 September 1968.

Wanstead was recorded as *Waenstede* in 1066 and the name is derived from the Old English *waen*, 'waggon' and *stede*, 'place'. It seems that there was once a ford here, where waggons crossed a stream, and 'stede' usually meant a holy place—therefore *Wanstead* means—'the holy place, near the ford crossed by waggons'.

The station was opened on 14 December 1947.

Wapping was recorded as *Wappinges* in 1231. There is a wide choice of possible meanings of this name. The first element could be from the Old English (1) *Wap*, 'a knock' or 'thump', (2) *Wapp*, 'a ship's rope', (3) *Wapel*, 'pool or mire', (4) *Wase*, 'mud', (5) a personal name of a Saxon *Waeppa*, all these with the Old English place name word ending *ing* literally 'the people who lived at'—presumably meaning 'the home of Waeppa's people'. Recorded as *Wapping Marshe* in 1562.

The station was opened as Wapping & Shadwell on 7 December 1869; renamed Wapping 10 April 1876; first used by Underground trains on 1 October 1884.

Warren Street. The estate in this area was owned by Charles Fitzroy, created Baron Southampton in 1780, and who married Anne, the daughter of Sir Peter *Warren*. When the street was named in 1799 it was called *Warren Street* in her honour.

The station was opened as Euston Road on 22 June 1907 and was renamed Warren Street on 7 June 1908.

Warwick Avenue. Many of the streets in the old manor of Paddington are connected with families who leased land from the Bishop of London. The original lessee was Sir John Frederick of Burwood in Surrey. His great-grandson married Jane *Warwick* of Warwick Hall in Cumberland in 1778 and the street is named in her honour.

The station was opened on 31 January 1915.

Waterloo was named in commemoration of the Battle of *Waterloo* (1815). The name was also given to the new bridge over the River Thames (originally called Strand Bridge) which was opened by the Prince Regent on 18 June 1817, the second anniversary of the Battle. The name was adopted for the main-line station opened on 11 July 1848, and later for the locality.

The Underground station was opened on 10 March 1906.

Watford was recorded in 944 and the name is derived from the Old English *waed,* 'place for wading' or *wad,* 'hunting'—and means 'ford which is used by hunters', from a once nearby natural feature.

The station was opened on 2 November 1925.

Watford High Street—see Watford.
Was recorded as *le High streate* in 1606 and is now part of the modern shopping centre.

The station was opened by the London & North Western Railway on 1 October 1862 and first used by Underground trains on 16 April 1917.

Waterloo Bridge (Embankment or Waterloo)

Watford Junction—see Watford.
Takes its name from the railway *junction* at this point.

The first station was opened by the London & Birmingham Railway on 20 July 1837 and resited in 1858. First used by Underground trains on 16 April 1917.

Wembley Central was recorded as *Wemba lea* in 825 and the name is derived from the personal name *Wemba* and the Old English *leah*, 'forest clearing'—and means 'the clearing where Wemba lived'. This name may be a nickname or could be taken from *Wemba*, the name of a Gothic King. It has had various spellings until recorded as *Wembley* in 1535.

The station was first used for Underground trains as Wembley for Sudbury on 16 April 1917; renamed Wembley Central 5 July 1948. A station called Sudbury was opened by the London & Birmingham Railway in 1842. It was renamed Sudbury & Wembley on 1 May 1882 and Wembley for Sudbury on 1 November 1910.

Wembley Park—see Wembley.
The station was opened on 12 May 1894.

West Acton—see Acton Town.
The station was opened on 5 November 1923.

Westbourne Park was recorded as *Westburn* in 1222 and is derived from the Old English *westan* and *burnam*, 'place'—means 'the place west of the stream'. Paddington was the sister village on the east bank. The road here was an ancient lane winding through the old *Westbourne Farm*. The Green was recorded in 1680 hence the *Park*, now a road.
The station was opened on 1 February 1866.

West Brompton signifies *Broom Town* with suggestions of a wide common—and means 'the common with the broom trees, near a town'.
The station was opened on 12 April 1869.

West Finchley—see Finchley Central.
The station was opened by the London & North Eastern Railway on 1 March 1933 and first used by Underground trains on 14 April 1940.

West Ham was recorded as *Hamme* in 958 which signifies that this and *East Ham* were then only one geographical location and it was not until 1186 when the name *Westhamma* was recorded. The name is derived from the Old English *hamm*, 'a water meadow'—referring to the low-lying riverside meadow near the bend of the Thames.
(see also **East Ham**.)
   The station was opened as West Ham by the London Tilbury & Southend Railway on 1 February 1901 and was first used by Underground trains on 2 June 1902; renamed West Ham Manor Road 11 February 1924, and reverted to West Ham on 1 January 1969.

West Hampstead—see Hampstead.
The station was opened on 30 June 1879.

West Harrow—see Harrow-On-The-Hill.
The station was opened on 17 November 1913.

West Kensington—see Kensington.
The station was opened on 9 September 1874 as North
End (Fulham); renamed West Kensington 1 March
1877.

Westminster. By tradition the site of the Abbey was
first known as Torneia (785) and means 'thorn island',
being once a low lying islet regularly cut off from the
mainland at high tide. Recorded as *Westminster* in 785,
the name is derived from west and Old English
mynster, 'monastery' or 'church', the west because it
lies to the west of London. *Westminster Abbey* began
as a small church attached to a Benedictine monastery,
was rebuilt in the 11th century and completed in 1388.
The village of *Westminster* (a City since 1540) was
joined up to London in the 18th century.

The station was opened as Westminster Bridge on
24 December 1868; renamed Westminster 1907;
reconstructed station opened 12 November 1923.

Westminster Abbey (Westminster)

West Ruislip—see Ruislip.

The station was opened on 21 November 1948.

The station on the adjacent Western Region line was opened by the Great Western & Great Central Joint Committee on 2 April 1906 as Ruislip & Ickenham. It was renamed West Ruislip on 30 June 1947.

Whitechapel takes its name from the *white* stone *chapel* of St. Mary Matfelon, first built in 1329, then rebuilt three times, until bombed in 1940 and finally demolished in 1952. Today there is no trace of the church that gave its name to this district.

The station was opened on 10 April 1876; first used by Underground trains 1 October 1884.

White City. The sports stadium was opened in 1908 to house part of the Franco-British Exhibition. The strikingly white finish of the buildings, and the exhibits in the main hall (all of which were white), earned the stadium its name.

The Hammersmith & City Line station was opened on 1 May 1908, and the Central Line station on 14 May 1908, both as Wood Lane. The Central Line station was resited and both renamed White City 23 November 1947. The Hammersmith & City station was closed from 25 October 1959; since 1 November 1914 it had been used only on special occasions.

Willesden Green was recorded as *Willesdone Grene* in 1254 and was formerly a distinct hamlet. *Willesden* itself was recorded as *Willesdune* in 939 and is derived from the Old English *wiell*, 'spring' and *dun*, 'hill', and means—'hill of the spring', referring to a once nearby natural location. *Willesden* was the name adopted *c.* 1840 by the London & Birmingham railway from the earlier spelling of *Wilsdon*.

The station was opened on 24 November 1879.

Willesden Junction—see Willesden Green.

The name has its origin in the railway *junction* at this point.

The station was opened by the London & North Western Railway on 1 September 1866 and first used by Underground trains on 10 May 1915.

Wimbledon was recorded as *Wunemannedunne c.* 950 and is derived from the personal name of the Saxon *Winebeald* and *down,* 'a hill'—means 'the hill where Winebeald lived', with his family. It has had various spellings in the course of time until recorded as *Wimbledon* in 1211.

The terminal station was opened on 3 June 1889, but the original London & Southampton Railway station opened on 21 May 1838.

Wimbledon Park—see Wimbledon.
The Park is to the west of the station.

The station was opened on 3 June 1889.

Woodford, as the name suggests, means 'the ford by a wood', over the River Roding which runs through the district.

The station was opened by the Eastern Counties Railway on 22 August 1856 and first used by Underground trains on 14 December 1947.

Wood Green was recorded as *Wodegrene* in 1502 and was once a separate hamlet on the edge of Enfield Chase. As the name suggests, means, 'the wood by the green'.

The station was opened on 19 September 1932.

Woodside Park was recorded as *Fyncheley Wode* in 1468 and was part of the great Middlesex woodland area, and named *Woodside* in 1686—being at the side of the wood.

The station was opened by the Great Northern Railway on 1 April 1872 as Torrington Park, Woodside. It was renamed Woodside Park on 1 May 1882. First used by Underground trains on 14 April 1940.

NAMES OF UNDERGROUND STATIONS NOW CLOSED

	Opened	Closed
Brill	1872	1935
British Museum	1900	1933
Brompton Road	1906	1934
City Road	1901	1922
Down Street	1907	1932
Drayton Park	1904	1975*
Essex Road	1904	1975*
Granborough Road (formerly Grandborough Road)	1868	1936
King William Street	1890	1900
Lords (former St. John's Wood Road)	1868	1939
Marlborough Road	1868	1939
Quainton Road	1868	1963
St. Mary's	1884	1938
South Acton	1905	1959
South Kentish Town	1907	1924
Strand	1907	1973
Uxbridge Road	1869	1940
Verney Junction	1868	1936
Waddesdon (formerly Waddesdon Manor)	1897	1936
Waddesdon Road (formerly Waddesdon)	1871	1935
Westcott	1871	1935
Winslow Road	1868	1936
Wood Lane (later White City)	1908	1959
Wood Siding	1872	1935
Wotton	1871	1935
York Road	1906	1932

* Transferred to Eastern Region

BIBLIOGRAPHY

F. R. Banks: *The Penguin Guide to London,* Penguin Books, Middlesex, 1973

Gillian Bebbington: *London Street Names,* B. T. Batsford Ltd., London, 1972.

John Bromley: *The Armorial Bearings of the Guilds of London*, Frederick Warne & Co. Ltd., London, 1960.

Kenneth Cameron: *English Place Names*, B. T. Batsford Ltd., London, 1961.

Basil E. Cracknell: *Portrait of London River*, Robert Hale Ltd., London, 1968.

G. J. Copley: *English Place Names and their Origins*, David & Charles, Newton Abbot, 1968.

Eilert Ekwall: *The Concise Oxford Dictionary of English Place Names*, Oxford University Press, 1960.

Eilert Ekwall: *Street-Names of the City of London*, Oxford University Press, London, 1965.

Geoffrey Evans: *Kensington*, Hamish Hamilton, London, 1975.

Charles James Féret: *Fulham Old and New (Vol. 1)*, Simpkin Marshall Hamilton Kent & Co. Ltd., London, 1900.

John Field: *Discovering Place-Names*. Shire Publications, Tring, 1971.

Margaret Gellings, W. F. H. Nicolaisen and Melville Richards: *The Names of Towns and Cities in Britain*, B. T. Batsford Ltd., London, 1970.

Edward Gordon and A. F. C. Deeson: *The Book of Bloomsbury*, Edward Gordon (Arts) Ltd., London, 1950

J. E. B. Gover, A. Mawer and F. M. Stenton: *The Place Names of Surrey*, Cambridge University Press, 1934.

Henry A. Harben: *A Dictionary of London*, Herbert Jenkins Ltd., London, 1918,

J. Edward Hart: *London Oddities*, London Transport, London, 1974.

Godfrey James: *London the Western Reaches*, Robert Hale Ltd., London, 1950.

William Kent: *An Encyclopaedia of London*, J. M. Dent & Sons Ltd., London, 1970.

A. Mawer and F. M. Stenton: *The Place Names of Middlesex*, Cambridge University Press, 1942.

A. Mawer and F. M. Stenton: *The Place Names of Hertfordshire*, Cambridge University Press, 1938.

Arthur Mee: *The King's England—Essex,* Hodder
& Stoughton, London, 1966.

Arthur Mee: *The King's England—London North of
the Thames,* Hodder & Stoughton, London, 1972.

W. G. Moore: *The Penguin Encyclopaedia of
Places,* Penguin Books, Middlesex, 1971.

Douglas Newton: *London West of the Bars,* Robert
Hale Ltd., London, 1951

Nicholson's: *Footloose in London,* Robert Nicholson
Publications, London.

André Page: *What you should know about London,*
Midas Books, Tunbridge Wells, Kent, 1973.

P. H. Reaney: *The Place-Names of Essex,* Cambridge
University Press, 1935.

P. H. Reaney: *The Origin of English Place-Names,*
Routledge & Kegan Paul, London, 1961.

Michael Robbins: *Middlesex,* Collins, London, 1953.

Gordon Ross: *A History of County Cricket, Surrey,*
Arthur Barker Ltd., London, 1971.

Stuart Rossiter: *The Blue Guides—London,* Ernest
Benn, Ltd., Kent, 1973.

Lilian and Ashmore Russan: *Historic Streets of
London,* Simpkin Marshall Hamilton Kent & Co.
Ltd., London, 1923.

Al Smith: *Dictionary of City of London Street
Names,* David & Charles, Newton Abbot, 1970.

H. G. Stokes: *English Place-Names,* B. T. Batsford
Ltd., London, 1949.

Bruce Stevenson: *Middlesex,* B. T. Batsford Ltd.,
London, 1972.

Cuthbert Wilfrid Whitaker: *History of Enfield* (1911),
Enfield Preservation Society, reprint, 1969.

Guy R. Williams: *London in the Country,* Hamish
Hamilton, London, 1975.

Leonard F. Wise: *World Rulers,* Ward Lock Educa-
tional, Sterling Publishing Co. Inc., 1967.

John Wittich: *Discovering London Curiosities,* Shire
Publications Ltd., Aylesbury, 1973.

Pieter Zwart: *Islington: A History and Guide,* Sidg-
wick & Jackson, London, 1973.